CONTENTS

1)	Introduction to William Dean Howells	1
2)	Introduction to the Rise of Silas Lapham	7
3)	Textual Analysis	
	Chapter One	12
	Chapter Two	15
	Chapter Three	20
	Chapter Four	24
	Chapter Five	29
	Chapter Six	33
	Chapter Seven	36
	Chapter Eight	39
	Chapter Nine	47
	Chapter Ten	52
	Chapter Eleven	55
	Chapter Twelve	60
	Chapter Thirteen	64
	Chapter Fourteen	68
	Chapter Fifteen	72
	Chapter Sixteen	74
	Chapter Seventeen	77
	Chapter Eighteen	80

	Chapter Nineteen	82
	Chapter Twenty	86
	Chapter Twenty-One	90
	Chapter Twenty-Two	92
	Chapter Twenty-Three	95
	Chapter Twenty-Four	99
	Chapter Twenty-Five	103
	Chapter Twenty-Six	109
	Chapter Twenty-Seven	115
4)	Character Analyses	122
5)	Critical Opinion of the Rise of Silas Lapham	134
6)	Essay Questions and Answers	138
7)	Bibliography	144

BRIGHT NOTES

THE RISE OF SILAS LAPHAM BY WILLIAM DEAN HOWELLS

Intelligent Education

Nashville, Tennessee

BRIGHT NOTES: The Rise of Silas Lapham
www.BrightNotes.com

No part of this publication may be used or reproduced in any manner whatsoever without written permission, except in the case of brief quotations in critical articles and reviews. For permissions, contact Influence Publishers http://www.influencepublishers.com.

ISBN: 978-1-645425-40-3 (Paperback)
ISBN: 978-1-645425-41-0 (eBook)

Published in accordance with the U.S. Copyright Office Orphan Works and Mass Digitization report of the register of copyrights, June 2015.

Originally published by Monarch Press.
Randall Hughes Keenan, 1965
2019 Edition published by Influence Publishers.

Interior design by Lapiz Digital Services. Cover Design by Thinkpen Designs.

Printed in the United States of America.

Library of Congress Cataloging-in-Publication Data forthcoming.
Names: Intelligent Education
Title: BRIGHT NOTES: The Rise of Silas Lapham
Subject: STU004000 STUDY AIDS / Book Notes

INTRODUCTION TO WILLIAM DEAN HOWELLS

EARLY PERIOD

William Dean Howells was born in Martin's Ferry, Ohio, March 1, 1837. His formal schooling ended at the age of twelve, but he was not without a rich nourishment of literature that increased his appetite for learning. Howells' father, William Cooper Howells, was an Ohio printer and newspaper editor whose own love of good literature prompted him to read aloud to his children from such authors as Washington Irving and Sir Walter Scott. In the autobiographical *Years of My Youth* (1916), Howells remarks on the fact that as a child he was always reading when he was not playing.

In 1849, his father bought the Dayton Transcript, a newspaper which later failed. The family moved to a log cabin in Greene County, Ohio, with the hope of activating an old paper mill there. This proved unsuccessful also, but Howells wrote of this period in *My Year in a Log Cabin* (1893), later to be included in *Years of My Youth*. In 1852 Howells' father became editor of the Sentinel, soon moving his family to the city of Jefferson; it was here that the young Howells contributed stories to the family paper. By 1855 he was contributing to such newspapers as the National Era, and the Ohio Farmer, becoming in the late 1850's an editor and writer on the *Ohio State Journal*. He read widely in such a variety of writers as Alexander Pope, Heinrich Heine, and Miguel de Cervantes. At this time also, he began to contribute to the *Atlantic Monthly*, thus beginning a long and influential association with that magazine.

The year 1860 saw two ambitious publications by Howells. With a young printer named John James Piatt, he published his first book, *Poems of Two Friends*. He also wrote a campaign biography of Abraham Lincoln that year, and in 1861 was appointed as a consul to Venice, Italy. The following year he was married in Paris to Elinor Gertrude Mead, a Vermont girl. He returned to the United States in 1865, but he had already been contributing to the *Boston Advertiser* and the *North American Review*. The first of Howells' many travel books, Venetian Life, was published in 1866, the same year that he assumed the post of assistant editor of the *Atlantic Monthly* in Boston. In 1867 the man who had ended his formal education at the age of twelve was awarded a Master of Arts degree by Harvard University and was University Lecturer in Italian Literature there from 1869 to 1871, at which time Howells was appointed editor of the *Atlantic Monthly*. During his ten years as editor, Howells wrote six novels, among which were *A Chance Acquaintance* (1872), *A Foregone Conclusion* (1875), *The Lady of Aroostook* (1879), and *Dr. Breen's Practice* (1881). These were novels of manners and morals, and Howells was particularly interested in their examination in a Boston setting. He is not recognized as a major American novelist on the merits of these books which prompted only modest interest in their own time; for the realistic novels that lay ahead were to establish his greatness in American literature.

THE ENTRANCE INTO REALISM

In 1882 Howells was offered a professorship at Johns Hopkins University, one of several such opportunities that also included an offer from Harvard. Howells declined them all, announcing as his reason an unwillingness to risk his reputation as "a middling novelist on the chance of his turning out a poor professor, or none." In that same year he published *A Modern Instance*, and in 1885 *The Rise of Silas Lapham* appeared. Both of these great novels were first published in serial form in the Century magazine, and they presented accurate and non-sensational realistic pictures of New England life and the character of the people.

In 1886 Howells began a column, the "Editor's Study" for *Harper's Magazine*, continuing in that activity until 1891. A third great novel, *Indian Summer*, appeared in 1886 after a serialization in *Harper's*; along with *A Modern Instance* and *The Rise of Silas Lapham*, it is part of Howells' movement into strong anti-romantic **realism** and a social criticism.

CHRISTIAN SOCIALISM

In 1888 Howells published *Annie Kilburn*, a tale of a small New England town and the industrial unrest among factory workers there. His growing tendency toward socialistic ideas found expression in this novel, and his cry for social justice was even stronger in 1890 with the publication of *A Hazard of New Fortunes*, which he considered his best novel. Howells grew increasingly concerned with the conflicts of society and the problems born of great industrialization. From the appearance of Silas Lapham in 1885, Howells bent more and more toward a Christian Socialism, a theory which held that the common welfare could be improved by the governmental regulation of free enterprise and economic competition along guidelines of Christian ethical principles. When, in fact, he published *A Traveler From Altruria* in 1894, his Christian Socialism reached its full force in the expression of Howells' repugnance at the condition of industrialized civilization. The work originally appeared in essay form in *The Cosmopolitan* over a period of twelve months during 1892 and 1893. His bent for Christian Socialism is traceable to several sources, among which are his Quaker background, his early acquaintance with the writings of the Scandinavian theologian and philosopher, Emanual Swedenborg, and the influential thought of the great Russian novelist Leo Tolstoy.

In 1895 Howells began contributing to *Harper's Weekly* on a regular basis. *The Landlord at Lion's Head* appeared in 1897 and, typical of Howells, it dealt with New England and the unromantic abrasive effect of traditional social gentility in contact with the force of new social values. From 1900 to his death in 1920, William Dean Howells was again associated with *Harper's Magazine* in writing his ideas, opinions and social commentary for the "Easy Chair" section of that publication. Between 1901 and 1905, Howells received three honorary Doctor of Literature degrees from Yale, Oxford, and Columbia, respectively. His later years were marked by the publication of *Through the Eye of the Needle* (1907), which he called "a sequel" to *The Traveler From Altruria*. The book, along with *The Leatherwood God* (1916), is located in a frontier setting and perpetuates Howells' hopeful notions of an ideal society erected on the principals of Christian Socialism.

THE "DEAN OF AMERICAN LETTERS"

In 1908 at the age of seventy-one, he was elected as the first president of the American Academy of Arts and Letters. Two years later, Mrs. Howells died after forty years of marriage. On his seventy-fifth birthday, Princeton University honored him with the Degree of Doctor of Humane Letters. It was another great tribute to the man whose education was mostly self-acquired, who had grown up on Dickens, Thackery, and George Eliot, who loved Trollope and "the divine Jane" Austen - a man, who in his boyhood days, had gained command of five languages, and who had become known as the "dean of American letters."

William Dean Howells' literary output was enormous. After 1870 his writings poured out in a seemingly endless flow. He wrote novels, thirty-five in number, plays in forms from farce to tragedies and blank verse, travel books, short stories, reminiscences, critical essays and poetry. "The Sleeping Car" (1883) is notable among his one act comedies, and *Criticism and Fiction* (1891) is most important for Howells' realistic criticism. Among his volumes of reminiscences are *My Year in A Log Cabin* (1893), *Literary Friends and Acquaintances* (1900), *My Mark Twain* (1910), and *Years of My Youth* (1916). When William Dean Howells died in New York City on May 11, 1920, he was a man as significant as a literary arbiter as he was a novelist. He was a man who could not accept romanticism, sentimentalism and melodrama in literature over the "truthful treatment" of life and society. Howells was influential also in the development of other great literary figures of the time. It was he who presented the early writings of Mark Twain and Henry James in the pages of the Atlantic Monthly. He championed Emily Dickenson's poems; encouraged and influenced Stephen Crane; wrote on European literary realists such as Emile Zola,

Henrik Ibsen, and Leo Tolstoy; and celebrated the American novelist Frank Norris.

In his lifetime popular interest in Howells' work waned considerably. At present this major American novelist and critic is receiving more of the respect and attention that his work has the right to command. However, there were those who understood that his time would come. Among them was Henry James whose eloquent letter, read at Howells' seventy-fifth birthday dinner in 1912, states how a great contemporary estimated the "dean's" body of literature. James wrote that Howells' books

> ...make a great array, a literature in themselves, your studies of American life, so acute, so direct, so distinterested, so preoccupied but with the fine truth of the case... The real affair of the American case and character...the thrill and the charm of the common...the character and the comedy, the point, the pathos, the tragedy, the particular home-grown humanity under your eyes...your really beautiful time will come.

THE RISE OF SILAS LAPHAM

INTRODUCTION

In the Boston of the eighteen seventies, Silas Lapham is an example of the new breed of self-made millionaires. His father's Vermont farm had contained the raw material necessary to develop a fine grade of mineral paint and Lapham had developed his great business out of this humble beginning. Now fifty-five years old, his tasteless advertisements are to be seen everywhere; and he is branching out into the foreign markets. When he had need of capital for his growing business, Lapham had taken Milton K. Rogers as a partner, only to forcibly buy him out and prevent him from sharing in the enormous profits that were to come.

Silas appreciates the devotion and assistance of his wife, Persis, in the growth of his company; but the woman's conscience is stricken by her husband's treatment of Rogers and she reminds him of it repeatedly.

Living in an unfashionable section of Boston, the Laphams are prompted to begin construction of a new mansion on elegant Beacon Hill by their concern for the future of their two daughters. On a trip to Canada, Mrs. Lapham and her younger daughter Irene meet a handsome young Bostonian socialite and his mother and sisters. The meeting and subsequent visit of the Boston matron to the Laphams, stimulates Persis Lapham's social awareness.

While the house is being constructed, the family again encounters the young man, Tom Corey, at the building site; and the Laphams begin to suspect that he is interested in the very beautiful Irene. Silas Lapham is impressed with the young man and confides to his wife that he would like to see him in the paint business, an ambition thoroughly ridiculed by her. However, Tom Corey shares Lapham's interest in the paint operation and goes to his father with his plans. Bromfield Corey is a Boston Brahmin, or aristocrat, whose life of inactivity and artistic dabbling had been supported by wealth inherited from his father, a rich merchant named Phillips Corey. The elder Corey disapproves of Tom's proposal but does not openly oppose his son's venture because he believes it as good a way as any to earn money, if one has to. The Corey fortune had been seriously depleted in recent years; and Bromfield Corey's wife, Anna, and his two daughters, Lily and Nanny, represent a strong drain upon the money that remains. Having recently graduated from Harvard, and realizing the necessity of finding employment, Tom Corey finds Lapham's paint business attractive.

After an interview with Lapham, Tom is hired to attend to the company's foreign correspondence and takes to the job with competence and enthusiasm. Mrs. Lapham, while attracted to the idea of a match between Irene and Corey, is still skeptical about the young man's supposed interest in paint and suspects that he is chasing Irene. While his mother and sisters are away at fashionable Bar Harbour, Tom passes the summer months in frequent visits to the Lapham's unfashionable cottage at equally unfashionable Nantasket. When the Corey ladies return to Boston, Mrs. Corey is dismayed and apprehensive about the attachment her son is forming with the socially inferior Laphams. Mrs. Corey pays an afternoon visit to the Laphams where she is received by Persis Lapham and her older and plain looking daughter, Penelope. Mrs. Corey and Penelope develop a mutual dislike for one another almost immediately, and the girl is quick to detect Mrs. Corey's opinion of her family. In the evening, the Laphams are surprised to receive a dinner invitation from the Coreys. Nervously, Mrs. Lapham accepts; but Penelope refuses to attend.

During the following week, the Laphams prepare for the dinner, while Silas is miserable with indecision about the proper formal attire. When they arrive at the Corey's fashionable home, Mrs. Lapham offers a clumsy excuse for Penelope's absence, causing her great embarrassment. During the dinner, Irene is seated next to Tom Corey where they talk mostly about Penelope. For the most part, Silas is bewildered by the polite dinner conversation and drinks a great deal of wine. Later in the drawing room "Colonel" Lapham tells the gentlemen of his Civil War experience, becomes very drunk, and thoroughly disgraces himself.

At the office the next day, Silas debases himself in apologizing to Tom Corey for his drunken performance; and the young man is both revolted and touched by his employer's humility. Believing himself to have been unsympathetic toward Lapham's apology, Tom Corey arrives at the Lapham house in the evening to pay his respects to the Colonel. Penelope is home alone and is astonished when Corey confesses his love for her. Realizing that Irene loves Corey and believing that he has been coming to see her, Penelope forbids him to come again and forces him to agree to it. When Mrs. Lapham hears the news of Tom's proposal, she sends for Silas to come home early and together they visit the Rev. Mr. Sewell, a minister whom they had met at the Corey dinner party. His opinion reflects what they feel deep in their hearts: Penelope and Tom should not sacrifice their love for the sake of Irene's feelings. When Persis Lapham breaks the news to Irene, the girl receives it with bitter courage and leaves the following day with her mother for Lapham, the family home town that has been renamed in honor of Silas.

Meanwhile, the Lapham business is becoming financially insecure. Because of his wife's insistence that he should atone for the supposed wrong done to Milton Rogers, Silas has loaned his old partner twenty thousand dollars. When Rogers' financial operations became shaky Silas continued to back him. Now, his only security is some mills out west that Rogers had given him, but these are in danger of losing their value because of a railroad monopoly that could force their sale at a low price. Silas' famous mineral paint is in danger also. A new company in West Virginia has developed an inexpensive method of developing their paint that allows them to undersell the Lapham product considerably. Reacting to news of Silas' impending financial collapse, Tom Corey offers his entire fortune of thirty thousand dollars to help support Silas' sagging paint company. Lapham graciously refuses.

Colonel Lapham then consults James Bellingham, Tom's uncle whom he had met at the Corey dinner. Bellingham suggests that Silas declare bankruptcy, but the self-made millionaire stoutly refuses. To make matters worse, the Lapham's half-completed mansion burns to the ground without proper insurance coverage. Convinced that he may yet save his tottering business, Lapham attempts to negotiate with the West Virginia company. After deliberation, it is agreed that Silas will invest a large amount of capital and the two companies will merge. Unable to raise much money, Lapham is presented with an offer by Rogers, who says that some English buyers wish to purchase the western mill properties.

He meets the buyers and suspects them and Rogers of dishonesty. Despite an emotional appeal by Rogers to Lapham's wife, the Colonel overcomes the temptation to capitalize on his ex-partner's dishonesty in order to save his own fortunes. Lapham is then given more time by the West Virginians to raise money. He interests a wealthy investor in his company, but conscience forces him to tell the man the circumstances of his current business affairs. The man withdraws his offer, and Silas' company is forced into bankruptcy.

The Lapham family returns to the Vermont town of their origin where Silas continues to manufacture a special paint he once named in honor of his wife. After he joins and invests in the West Virginia paint company, Tom marries Penelope and they travel to Mexico where Tom is to operate a paint company office. After several years Irene is still unmarried, the Coreys still maintain their aristocratic aloofness, and Silas has acquired a philosophic resignation to the loss of his great fortune.

THE RISE OF SILAS LAPHAM

TEXTUAL ANALYSIS

CHAPTER ONE

....

The year is 1875; and in the office of Silas Lapham, Boston millionaire and paint manufacturer, a young reporter, Bartley Hubbard, begins to interview the industrialist for a series of newspaper sketches on the "Solid Men of Boston." Lapham is a thick-set hulk of a man, medium in height, with a forceful, determined chin. His shoulders are "massive" and his forehead wide and formidable. He wears a "reddish-grey" beard, in the male fashion of the day; and his eyes are blue, reflecting the gentleness or severity of his mood.

In the course of Hubbard's interview, Lapham reminisces widely about his birth fifty-five years ago and his youth on his father's Vermont farm. Bored by observations on Lapham's hard-working, self-sacrificing mother, the reporter steers the interview to the subject of the special paint that Lapham manufacturers. When he was a boy, his father had discovered a "paint-mine" on their farm, but could never develop it into a business. After his parents' deaths, Lapham maintained the farm for sentimental values. He did not remain there but went off to Texas. Soon tiring of the West, he returned to Vermont, settling in the town of Lumberville. He handled horses at a hotel, bought a stage and "run the business myself," owned a tavern, and eventually married the town schoolteacher. With the encouragement of his wife, Persis, Lapham developed the "paint-mine" into a business.

During the Civil War, he served with the Union Army, rising to the rank of colonel and receiving a leg wound at the battle of Gettysburg. When the war ended, Lapham expanded his paint business. He had a pressing need for capital; and at the insistence of his wife, he entered into a partnership with a man who had money but knew nothing about paint. After "a year or two," Lapham forced him out and went on alone to harvest the profits of the business. Now, the business is an international success with offices all over the world; and Lapham's faith in his product is so great that he considers it "a blessing to the world."

After the interview, the cynical and amused Hubbard is driven in Lapham's carriage to the young reporter's office; on the way, they discuss their mutual interest in fine horses. Writing with a sense of "inward derision," Hubbard's sketch of the Boston millionaire is overly flattering and extravagant. He is an example of "single-minded purpose and unwavering perseverance," the sketch reads, and is certainly 'one of nature's noblemen."

When he arrives home Bartley Hubbard effects a thoroughly superior attitude about Lapham. In his account of the interview to his wife, Marsha, he says that he only wishes that decency had allowed him to say what he really thought of the man and his "landscape advertising" with colored paints. Hubbard discovers that a parcel has been sent to them. It contains a jar of "Persis Brand," Colonel Lapham's best quality paint, named in honor of his wife. Marsha Hubbard is delighted and thinks that her husband has bought it for her as a surprise. Hubbard quickly destroys the illusion and announces that "The old fool's sent it to you" as a gift. Marsha remarks on Lapham's goodness and asks her husband not to make fun of him "as you do some of those people." Hubbard's glib answer is that the ridicule would never be the sort that Lapham would ever realize.

> Comment: Chapter one is a chapter of exposition. Howells uses the interview by Bartley Hubbard as a device for revealing Lapham's background to the reader. It is an effective method for it provides us with the man's history in his own words, and by doing so, introduces us to this Boston millionaire as a personality. Bartley and Marsha Hubbard make their first and only appearance here in chapter one. However, Howells' passing reference to future difficulties between the couple refers to their disastrous marriage as found in *A Modern Instance*, an 1882 novel by Howells in which they are principal characters.
>
> During the interview, Lapham remarks boastfully about the durability and protective qualities of his mineral paint. Hubbard inquires humorously whether he ever thought of testing it on the human conscience. Silas replies, "No, sir... I guess you want to keep that as free from paint as you can, if you want much use of it. I never cared to try it on mine."
>
> The remark appears to be merely a part of Lapham's expansive ramble about the virtues of that "blessing," his paint; but we shall discover later in the book that the comment is significant. For Silas Lapham, the mineral paint discovered on his father's farm is more than a commercial product; it is a matter of faith.

THE RISE OF SILAS LAPHAM

TEXTUAL ANALYSIS

CHAPTER TWO

....

Lapham drove home to Nankeen Square at the South End of Boston. He had gotten the house "...very cheap of a terrified gentleman of good extraction who discovered too late that the South End was not the thing...." Silas and his wife were very satisfied with their bargain and had lived there for twelve years. The summer before the story begins, Mrs. Lapham and her daughter Irene were in Canada, where by chance they met other Bostonians - a mother and two daughters. Some of their luggage was lost, and the mother became very ill. Mrs. Lapham nursed the woman and lent her and her daughter some clothing. The woman's son soon arrived and expressed great thanks for all that Mrs. Lapham and her daughter had done. Mrs. Lapham thought him to be the nicest young man about. She had small grounds for comparison; for despite the Lapham's great wealth, they enjoyed no social life in Boston. In their unsophisticated country ways, they spent their newly acquired wealth on expensive but ugly clothing and furnishings; "but they did not know how to spend on society." An occasional tea for neighborhood ladies and a "pot-luck" supper for one of Lapham's good customers provided their only "social life." The two daughters had attended the public school but had avoided attending the finishing school, which their mother had encouraged, for fear of being snubbed socially. Lapham was just as pleased, for he considered that they had acquired education enough.

They were not "accomplished" girls, however. They had taken dancing lessons but not instruction in the socially acceptable private classes; they were not aware that such things even existed. The daughters and their mother kept much to themselves. They passed hours shopping, napping, or discussing what they had seen from their window over Nankeen Square. The younger daughter, Irene, was very beautiful, was extremely competent at housework, and was fond of shopping and taking care in her dress. Penelope was the older daughter by three years. She read extensively, attended many lectures about which she could always provide a humorous account, and "…could make fun of nearly everything…." Irene was lovely but innocent to a fault, while Penelope, dark and plain in appearance, had a quick and intelligent mind.

When Irene met the young Bostonian in Canada, it was an unaccustomed experience; for she had until then relied upon her mother and sister for her opinions and reactions to everything. Therefore, she was conscious of every detail about the young man's actions and discussed them carefully when the family returned to Boston and Nankeen Square. Indulging in some wishful thinking, Mrs. Lapham interpreted the affair to her husband as a possible indication of interest in Irene by the young man. She remarked on the family's fine manners and how extensively they had traveled. When Colonel Lapham heard the name of the family his wife and daughter had met, he remarked that they were idlers and were not engaged in any business at all. They were very nice people, commented Mrs. Lapham, and the Colonel countered with the fact that they should be - "They never done anything else."

During the winter, the ladies of the family in question paid a late afternoon call upon the Laphams. They were so late in arriving, said the mother, because their friends lived "...on the New Land or on the Hill," and they were not familiar with this section of Boston. It was a bit of social snubbing and the Lapham women dwelt upon it for some time. When told of the visit and the remark Lapham commented that he owned some property up on the Back Bay area where the socially prominent Boston families lived. "Want me to build on it?", he questioned humorously. After struggling with herself about the matter and the possibility of its offering the girls better opportunities socially, Mrs. Lapham decided against building a new house. The next morning at breakfast, Mrs. Lapham asked her daughters if they would like their father to build on the "New Land." The girls were unenthusiastic; Persis Lapham was relieved and spoke no more about it.

Months passed and finally an appeal for a contribution to charity arrived from their new acquaintances on Beacon Hill. Silas wrote a check for five hundred dollars, but his wife tore it up and substituted one for one hundred dollars. We don't want to show off, snapped Mrs. Lapham, but her husband said he thought perhaps she did. The topic of a new house arose once again, but Mrs. Lapham still maintained that she did not want to build. However, she suggested that perhaps he was the one that really wanted the new house all along. Affectionately, Silas Lapham agreed. Driving down Beacon Street, in their horsedrawn sleigh, the Colonel remarked that their daughters would look elegant sitting behind a large paned window such as those in the socially prominent homes along the way; and his wife agreed. After giving his frisky horse a long run, Silas turned to his wife and declared that he had nearly made up his mind to build on their Back Bay lot. Don't do it because of me, was Persis Lapham's response.

Back at Nankeen Square, Penelope, or Pen as she was called, agreed in her curious, half-serious manner, that it was a good idea. What is money for, she added, if you can't enjoy it? The matter seemed to be decided, even though Silas Lapham appeared to be the least serious of all - but that was his way, as the girls had often remarked.

> **Comment: Chapter two acquaints us with the remaining members of the Lapham family, and we begin to see their relationship to the exclusive Boston society and its attitude toward them. The Laphams are rich but without the accomplishments and social graces that distinguish the aristocratic families of Boston society. Their taste in apparel and in the furnishings of their home is coarse and unbecoming. The daughters, Penelope and Irene, opposite in personalities, are both "unfinished" according to the standards of society; and the parents themselves are little changed from their days in the farm country of northern Vermont. The seeds of social discontent have now been planted by the hands of the elegant Boston family whom Irene and her mother met in Canada, a family we shall come to know as the Coreys and one that typifies Boston aristocracy for Howells. Mrs. Corey's visit and remark about her unfamiliarity with Nankeen Square has prompted Persis Lapham, reluctant as she would be to admit it, to think more and more about the social unacceptability of their present address. As unsophisticated as they are,**

they wish to provide the best possible advantages for their daughters. Silas Lapham displays a pride as fierce and formidable as the social consciousness of the Boston aristocracy. He is vigorously alert to the fact that he is what he is by his own labor. His life is one of energy and personal accomplishment rather than the one of idleness and basking leisure that he associates with the Coreys when his wife mentions their gentility.

In this chapter we see the homely artless way in which the Laphams engage each other. Their almost gruff directness, as Howells remarks, is a characteristic of a type of personal warmth and confidence. It is charming and the deep affection between Lapham and his wife is not hidden, but its roughness is typical of those rooted ways that separate this self-made millionaire and his family from the fashionable Boston world about them.

THE RISE OF SILAS LAPHAM

TEXTUAL ANALYSIS

CHAPTER THREE

....

As the winter drew to a close, Irene Lapham received a newspaper from Texas. It contained an account of a large ranch there, but was unaccompanied by any explanatory note. Mrs. Lapham, however, surmised that it must surely be from that young man, Tom Corey, whom they had met in Canada, and who was staying in Texas for a time. Irene clipped the account and fastened it to the mirror in her room. When the spring arrived Silas Lapham proved that he was in earnest about a new house by consulting an architect, Mr. Seymore, about the plans. Seymore diplomatically concealed his shock upon hearing the grotesque details of Lapham's plans for the home he wished built. Gradually, the architect directed the Laphams' choices in design and appointments toward the elegant and tasteful. Silas was impressed with the man as he was with anyone who could meet him with authority on an issue, and Persis remarked that he knew what a woman wanted in a house "better than she does herself."

The house that would overlook the bay was not begun until late in April, and construction seemed to creep along. Lapham, himself, took the greatest satisfaction in watching the pile driving, and he followed it with the fascination of a child. By late April or early May, the great houses in the neighborhood had been boarded up for the summer and the families gone to one of the fashionable summer resorts on Cape Cod.

It was the custom of Mrs. Lapham and her daughters to vacation at Nantasket, one of the less fashionable locations. This summer had provided the fascination of the new house, so they had lingered longer than usual.

Following the interview with Bartley Hubbard, Silas had dropped him at the offices of his newspaper, Events. He had driven out to the new house with Persis, but something happened to dampen the joy they usually experienced. As they dismounted from their carriage, they met Milton K. Rogers, Lapham's former partner whom he had bought off and forced from the paint business. The exchange that followed was cold and incompatible, with Mrs. Lapham and Rogers exchanging only stiff pleasantries. Silas remained silent. "I had nothing to say to him," he offered later. Persis then began berating her husband for what she believed to be the ruthless and ungrateful way in which he had driven Rogers out of the business years before. She can never forget it, she declares, and can never help but believe that her husband has ruined the man. The subject had always been a tender one, with Persis believing a moral wrong had been committed and Silas maintaining that his conscience was clear. He never wanted a partner in the first place, but then Rogers' money had saved him from complete loss. He had forced the partner out of the business without a real choice, even though the man took away more money than he put in. Lapham was saved by Rogers' money but the man had no love for the product (the way Silas did) and would have pulled the business down sooner or later; he simply did not belong. "You had made paint your god," Mrs. Lapham lamented, "and you couldn't bear to let anybody else share in its blessings."

Lapham wished to hear no more of the matter and told his wife not to meddle. She refused and said that she would always do so when she saw him "hardening" himself in such wrongdoing. Silas replied that he felt no guilt in the matter, for he had simply relieved himself of a partner "that didn't know anything, and couldn't do anything." Persis Lapham flared back at her husband with the charge that he had driven Rogers out when he knew that the business would soon be worth twice its value. You took his share too, she added, and that was why you avoided looking at him when we met. Lapham raged and turned the carriage for home, with Persis vowing never to live in the new house - "There's blood on it."

Comment: This is an important chapter in the development of the story for several reasons. The clipping from the newspaper that Mrs. Lapham and Irene believe has been sent by Tom Corey is the first rung in a ladder of misconception that leads the sisters and young Corey to the pain of heartbreak. Construction on the house has begun and as the building rises, with its tasteful decor, it seems to symbolize their prosperity and the attempt of the Laphams, whether they would admit it or not, to grow up and out of their Lumberville, Vermont, ways. This symbol of their prosperity then clashes with something that helped bring it about. The meeting with Milton Rogers in front of the construction

serves to bring the affair with the partner plainly before the reader. It also provides a glimpse into a particular side of Persis Lapham that sits like a sore wound ready to be opened from time to time. The fact that Silas forced Rogers out of the business has preyed upon her conscience, and she believes it must surely torment her husband's, if he would only confess to it. It is a nearly puritanical sense of guilt and moral wrong that Persis Lapham is afflicted with. More than a sense of justice violated, it grows out of proportion, gnawing away at her until she cannot rest nor allow Silas to forget. As the novel advances she will be the voice of her husband's conscience in this matter; we will discover that the price for appeasing her scrupulous moral sense is a costly one.

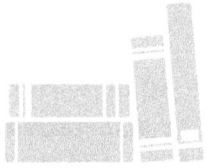

THE RISE OF SILAS LAPHAM

TEXTUAL ANALYSIS

CHAPTER FOUR

Howells commences chapter four with more **exposition** of the Laphams' past. People such as these, he observes, "do not weigh their words." They are blunt, while the jabs and calculated exchanges of refined speech are unknown to them. Persis Lapham had been a schoolteacher and her marriage to Silas has given him a "rise in life." She was a clearheaded woman, uncomplaining, "with sense and principle," and strove always to do what was "wise and right." Early in the marriage they had lost a son, and it had affected them deeply. After the war, when Silas began to expand his paint business, Persis had been "the spring of his enterprise" by the strength of her zeal and courage. In the troublesome matter with Rogers, she possessed that wifely quality of accusing loyalty; urging him to set his wrongdoing to rights, she yet would have defended him against his own self-accusations. The temptation to force out a man had become useless to the business but whose money had saved it, was a mighty one - and one above which Silas Lapham was not able to "rise." He could always satisfy himself about the matter, except during those times when his wife would drag it up anew. It appeared to lie quietly for a while, but with "unextinguishable vitality," it never seemed to die.

It was the Lapham's custom to ignore quarrels without bothering to require any "explicit reconciliation." It was natural, therefore, that after a few days Persis Lapham would suggest that the girls might like to drive over to the new house. It was equally appropriate that Silas would suggest that they all go along.

While their mother explored the semi-completed house, the Lapham girls suddenly caught sight of young Tom Corey. Elegantly dressed and handsomely tanned from his recent Texas visit, he had stopped in Boston on his way to Bar Harbour to see his mother and sisters. He was introduced to the Colonel who led him about the house expounding loudly and boastfully on its grandeur, cost, and his own wisdom in selecting such a fine architect. The girls suffered embarrassment at their father's bragging but were rescued from it by the appearance of Mrs. Lapham from a floor above. After an exchange of pleasantries and a clumsy invitation by Lapham, the family drove back to Nankeen Square.

That evening, Silas commented that he could "make a man" of the young Corey fellow if he had him in his business, despite his society background and fine education. The girls also discussed Tom Corey. Irene was taken with the young man more than ever now, and coyly encouraged her sister's teasing about Corey, while at the same time pretending torment from it. She mused on his close-cropped hair and the turn of his nose, while Penelope declared facetiously that he must be a man of superior judgment based, of course, on the good taste he displayed in his clothes. The girls soon fell to humorous imitations of the Colonel in his pompous boasting to Corey, and their "nervous shrieks" of delight soon routed their father, who complained that they should go to bed.

> **Comment:** In the first pages of this chapter, Howells uses the word "rise' twice, once in connection with Silas' marriage and again in reference to his inability to overcome the temptation of forcing Rogers out of the business. The use of this word is significant because it opens a fresh dimension in the meaning of the book's title for the reader. Howells is beginning to build the idea of a moral rising and falling in Lapham, related to a material prosperity and loss. Persis "had tried to be his conscience," observes Howells, and this is the moving agency that will work upon the man toward a correction of his ethical lapse. The question of Roger's treatment is not really one of dishonesty, but rather one of ethics and integrity. For Persis with her puritanical sense of moral justice that must see blame fixed and all wrongs put right, an act of questionable business integrity has grown to a great moral burden that weighs all the heavier upon her shoulders because it seems to weigh so lightly upon her husband's.
>
> This chapter is equally significant for the beginning of the love triangle between Tom Corey and Lapham sisters. Irene is romantically and idyllically taken with the handsome young Bostonian; she makes no pretense of it to her sister and, in a proper and shy way, hints the same to Corey. If we read carefully, we cannot avoid sensing a mutual awareness beginning to take hold between Corey and "Pen" Lapham as well. Between

the light banter and polite conversation, the older of the Lapham girls and the young Harvard graduate seem to be all too conscious of one another. To Corey's remark that it must be exciting to build a house, Pen merely agreed, "loyally refusing in Irene's interest the opportunity of saying any more." As they spoke, "Corey looked at her, and saw that she was shorter than her sister, and had a dark complexion." Irene is beginning to lose Corey's attention and in his remark to her that Pen "seems to have a good deal of humour," there is just the hint of preoccupation with the older girl.

When the girls discuss the afternoon meeting in their room at Nankeen Square, Irene is the one whose giddiness is taken up with the superficial appearance of Corey, his short hair, his well-tailored jacket and the slope of his nose. Pen's replies are good humored and teasingly calculated to please her eager sister. We can see strong differences here between the two sisters. Irene, innocent and fluttering about in a first love, is no more than she should be in the situation. As for Penelope, her jesting responses to her sister's excited speculations about Corey are those of a person who acts for the sake of another. She is more intelligent than her sister, and her reactions to life are quieter, less openly emotional, but strikingly blunt in a humorous way. Pen admits to Corey's good looks and observes that he has "very good eyes." Irene offers only momentary attention to this more expressive aspect of the young man and titters on excitedly about the cut of his "sack coat."

On the way back from the new house Colonel Lapham remarks that he should prefer to see a young man "act like a man" and not be supported and cared for by his wealthy father. The colonel speculates that young Corey probably belongs to several clubs and spends his days in idle gazing out of their windows. Pen quickly snaps back that if she were a man she would belong to "twenty clubs" and look out of the windows until she "dropped." This defiance was the girl's humorously irreverent way of reacting to her father's blustering; however, the suspicion is there also that it is at least an unconscious defense of a young man who is beginning to occupy her thoughts.

THE RISE OF SILAS LAPHAM

TEXTUAL ANALYSIS

CHAPTER FIVE

At the same time that the Lapham sisters were sorting out Tom Corey's finer points, the young man arrived at the Corey home in fashionable Boston. He and his father, Bromfield Corey, discussed the absence of friends and neighbors during the long summer months and then lighted upon the topic of young Corey's future. The family fortune had seen brighter days and Tom Corey could not now pass a life of ease and idleness in the manner of his father. Tom was cold to the idea of marrying for money if money was to be the only consideration. Bromfield Corey maintained that "the affections could be made to combine pleasure and profit." A rich girl would be less ambitious and uneasy, since she would have had all the advantages during her life. It would be important, however, offered Tom, that her family have been wealthy long enough to guarantee her some social position or else her lot, in this respect, would be no better than some poor girl's. With wealth, lamented the father, the "suddenly rich" are on a plane with us. Money is most important now and has the power to claim position at once. It is "the romance, the poetry of your age," he tells his son, but the situation really does not disturb him. Nevertheless, a bit of beauty, some good sense, an awareness of good conduct - and a decently grammatical way of speaking would be acceptable in a wife.

The father and son then discussed the Laphams. Tom Corey submitted that the Colonel was a rather ungrammatical person, but that despite his "syntax," he rather liked him. Following a brief comment on social aristocrats and commoners, the conversation turned once more to young Corey's prospects, with the son expressing his hopes of entering Lapham's mineral paint business. I am going to think it over, Tom remarked, and then go down to Lapham's office and explore the matter with him. The father did not fully agree with the plan, nor did he fully disagree, but said humorously that it was consoling to think that while he had been idly spending and enjoying himself, he had also been laying the path of "industry and self-reliance" for his son.

A portrait of Bromfield Corey's father hung over the mantle and the resemblance between it and Tom Corey was evident, particularly in the shape of his "Roman" nose. The grandfather had been a vastly successful India merchant whose business hopes for his son Bromfield never materialized. With a modest talent as an artist, young Bromfield had traveled about Europe, eventually settling in Rome. There he lingered, "rounding" the sharpness of his aristocratic background into a gentle Italianate smoothness. He continued to dabble in painting, married socially, and soon had his own son "on his hands." It is a shame, Bromfield Corey observed with half-seriousness, that you have your grandfather's nose, or else you would "go and travel as I did."

As the Laphams retired for the night at Nankeen Square, Silas repeated his earlier conviction that if he had Tom Corey in the paint business with him he would surely "make a man of him." He would have nothing to do with mineral paint, Persis replied with authority. To her husband's puzzled question as to just why she should think not, she answers that there is no sense in telling him if he does not already know.

> **Comment:** Having introduced the socially graceless Lapham family, Howells now allows us a greater knowledge of the character and personality of Tom Corey and his genteel father. We see that Tom Corey has some practicality about him, that his sense of social democracy is a bit flexible, but that his aristocratic lineage does not permit him to completely embrace the Laphams. However, he is intelligent enough to recognize and respect in Silas Lapham the personal drive and ability that has lifted his Vermont paint business into an international industry. Tom's levelheadedness brings to his attention the need to provide a future for himself. With the lessening of the Corey wealth, the need becomes even stronger. Regardless of the ebbing Corey finances, it is evident that Tom's character requires him to forge his own way in the world. When the Lapham girls teased and tittered about his "Roman" nose, it seemed simply an addition by Howells of one more piece of realistic detail. It is that certainly, but it is also our visible sign of Tom's inheritance from his merchant grandfather of traits more energetic and ambitious than those of his own father. In the portrait of the old Corey, Bromfield sees the same facial characteristics and realizes that it is significant of a legacy of strong character and will. Tom Corey was searching for a way to follow in life, and as Howells observes, "He had the Roman nose and the energy without the opportunity...."

In the person of Bromfield Corey, Howells provides an agreeable but idle aristocratic dilettante. He is pleasantly articulate and his gracefulness is a combined result of breeding, travel, personal cultivation, and associations. He is wittily philosophic and his approach to life is remarkably undeluded and realistic. Bromfield Corey makes no undue pretensions. He is calmly aware of his patrician heritage as well as his lack of accomplishment in life. This lifetime of casual interest and prolonged idleness he can distinguish as one of the choices available to those whose family wealth provides an opportunity for an uncomplicated and tasteful existence.

In the closing lines of the chapter, we see that Lapham's casual remark about bringing Tom Corey into the business has become something of a preoccupation. It seems reasonable to suspect, however, that as a father anxious for his daughter's future, Silas Lapham is not unconscious of a possible match between Corey and Irene.

THE RISE OF SILAS LAPHAM

TEXTUAL ANALYSIS

CHAPTER SIX

....

The Corey family had always maintained a summer home at Nahant; but after renting for a while, they saw that they could do without it. Young Tom Corey realized that the family's financial circumstances were in such a condition that if they did not take some care to economize, they would soon be reduced to an unaccustomed way of living. Therefore, the summer house was sold. The Corey girls and their mother now summered at Bar Harbour, and this is where Tom traveled to visit them. He informed them that he had found nothing suitable for a future occupation on his Texas trip and mentioned his idea about the mineral paint business. The crudeness of Lapham's advertisements immediately came to Mrs. Corey's mind and she admitted that the prospect of such employment seemed "distasteful" to her. "It's not only the kind of business," she added, "but the kind of people you would be mixed up with." To her son's additional remark that the Laphams were building a home "on the water side of Beacon Street," Mrs. Corey returned with the observation that it was becoming "very common down there."

On his return to Boston, Tom Corey presented himself at Silas Lapham's office and declared his hope of entering the business. Colonel Lapham was stunned and would have squandered any amount simply to have his wife present to hear Corey's proposition. Corey added that he did not really know where he could fit in, since his view of the business had been an outside one. With a touch of uneasiness showing through, Lapham minimized the biographical sketch of him done by Bartley Hubbard in the Events, and hoped that Corey had not been led by it to any false conclusions about the business. No, said Corey politely, he did not read the Events regularly and did not know what the colonel meant.

Lapham was impressed with the young man's knowledge of foreign languages and his willingness to sell the paint abroad on a commission basis. After testing his sincerity for a while and responding visibly to young Corey's declaration that "I believe in" the paint, Lapham launched an enthusiastic account of his product's origin and invited the young man along to the family's summer bungalow at Nantasket. On the steamboat ride across the bay, young Corey was anxious to talk business but could only extract homely philosophy, political comments and idle talk from the talkative Colonel. When the boat docked, they were met by Penelope Lapham in a horse-drawn beach wagon. Colonel Lapham took the reins, offered his daughter "a wink of supreme content" and drove off toward the bungalow. When they arrived, the aroma of supper was in the air and Mrs. Lapham was on the veranda.

> **Comment: In this chapter Tom Corey demonstrates some of his more practical and ambition side, inherited from his grandfather. We are given an opportunity to become more acquainted with Mrs. Corey, aristocratic like her husband, but more**

aggressively conscious of it than he is. She is amiably displeased at the thought of her son's placement in Colonel Lapham's paint business but retains her aristocratic bearing.

In Colonel Lapham's enthusiasm for his paint, his invitation to Corey, and the buggy trip to the cottage, we see Silas' almost boyish enthusiasm and his open display of natural good spirits. The trip to the Lapham's cottage at Nantasket opens the way for closer contact between Corey and the Laphams, and provides for a deepening of the relationship between the three young people.

THE RISE OF SILAS LAPHAM

TEXTUAL ANALYSIS

CHAPTER SEVEN

With some self-satisfaction. Silas announced to his wife the purpose of young Corey's visit, but the woman would not be convinced. Later in the evening, Irene, who had remained in her room with a headache, joins the rest of the family and their guest. The young people discuss literature and, in particular, the novel Middlemarch by George Eliot, a library copy of which is lying upon a table. It soon becomes evident that Pen and Tom Corey have a mutual interest in literature. Despite Pen's efforts to support her younger sister in the conversation, the fact remains that Irene does not share in the literary interests. Silas joins the discussion, confessing to precious little time for reading books, but admitting to an interest in lectures and the theater. Mrs. Lapham returns the conversation to literature. She read some good books when she was a girl, she says, but her own mother frowned upon novels, calling them nothing but "lies." Yes, replies, Corey, they certainly are "fictions." Whenever the girls want a novel, they can get it in the library; for after all, the Colonel offers, that's what libraries are for.

Lapham suggests that the young people take the night air on the beach. Wishing to talk with his wife, he is flushed with satisfaction that he was able to get them "out of the way." Persis Lapham is convinced that Corey has no real interest in the paint business and is only attentive for Irene's sake. Silas disagrees. He would not object to any interest Tom might show in Irene; but the boy is sincere, he maintains. He does not propose to allow anyone to deceive him, but he is certain that Corey "means paint first, last, and all the time." Persis is finally satisfied that young Corey wishes to enter the business, but she questions Silas' reaction should the boy fail to take an interest in their daughter. I know you are counting on it, she remarks with authority, and you'll be disappointed if the match fails to come off. Silas denies that he has "his heart set on it," but then admits that his wife knows more about what is on his mind than he does.

The Colonel then strolled out onto the veranda and could see his daughters and Tom Corey in the distance. As he gazed after them, he thought about the Coreys themselves. In his "simple, brutal" way, their name had always been a despised symbol of the grandeur and position that he could scarcely hope to discover in his own family for generations ahead. In the business world, he had heard of Tom's grandfather, Phillips Corey, and he was acquainted with the name and face of the old merchant's useless son, Bromfield. He had seen Bromfield Corey on one occasion, and the elegant and trim spectacle of the man had repelled him as the sum of all that was aristocratic.

In Tom Corey, all of Silas' prejudices disappeared. He thoroughly liked the boy. He had called Persis' notions about Tom and Irene a foolish "superstition," but he was now willing to admit that he shared it somewhat. As the distant figures turned back toward the house. Lapham hastily stepped inside to avoid their notice.

Comment: In their literary topics and conversation, Corey and Pen begin to move closer together, while the young man's interest in Irene fails to be sparked. Mrs. Lapham's hope for a match between her younger daughter and Corey has been self-convincing, and it has also been contagious. Some wishful thinking on Lapham's part and the conversation with his wife has stimulated his hopes for his daughter and Corey as well. The whole family is now rather well convinced of the possibility of an eventual marriage and the pattern has been laid for the disastrous heartbreak that is to come.

In his reminiscence about the Corey family, Lapham reveals his rough and instinctive antagonism as a self-made man for those who enjoy aristocratic wealth and position. The image of the idle and unproductive Bromfield Corey was enough to predispose Silas against his more satisfactory son. We can see, however, that Lapham is not blinded by prejudice, for he takes to the younger man because of his sincerity and spirited eagerness, perhaps reminiscent of his own long ago in the Vermont farm lands.

THE RISE OF SILAS LAPHAM

TEXTUAL ANALYSIS

CHAPTER EIGHT

A week after Tom Corey had informed his mother of his plans to enter the Lapham paint concern, Mrs. Corey returned to Boston from Bar Harbour to discuss the matter with her husband. It is a dreadful situation, she says, and asks why he did not put a stop to the thing. It might even be a good idea, replies Corey. After all, the boy has tried so many different ventures and come away from them all. He might even give this one up too, but I had no desire to interfere, he adds, since I had nothing to suggest in its place. I do not believe he will waste himself on the project. He has great energy, not brilliance, and he must do something. If the money earned is done so fairly and honestly, we should make no pretenses to caring about the source, since we really do not care after all. "That superstition is exploded everywhere." Besides this paint business affair, says Mrs. Corey, there is the matter of his marrying, and I do wish he had married someone. Someone with money, returns her husband. The elder Corey confesses to having tried to interest Tom in such an approach to marriage but has failed. I rather admire him for the quality, observes the father. If we consider the money side of it, we should remember that the "paint princess" will have a great deal in time. That makes it all the worse, objects Mrs. Corey. The girl is pretty enough, but she is "insipid; she is very insipid." Bromfield Corey admits that he is amazed at his own "hardihood" in the matter. Here is my son, obliged to make his living by a weakening of values. It is curious, he adds philosophically. Values in art never shrink, yet investments in such things as stocks and real estate are apt to. Pictures might be the very place to put all one's values, he jests. Mrs. Corey observes that there is really no need for Tom to earn a living at all. There is still enough to provide adequately for all of us. I have told Tom that very thing, returns Corey. Some careful economy could enable him to live out his days without ever doing anything. It might make things a bit close for the rest of us, but we must all make some sacrifices. He simply could not agree with me, even when I cited European gentry as examples of leisurely idleness. It seems, Corey offers with some droll wit, that Tom is simply "selfish."

Mrs. Corey smiled wistfully. It had been thirty years since she married "the rich young painter in Rome." He had a way of saying such charming things and they pleased the Boston girl with her practical and serious ways. Once they had returned to Massachusetts, his lovely way with words continued, but he remained idle. The truth of it is that Bromfield Corey had "fulfilled the promise of his youth."

He was never a wild and heedless spender. On the contrary, his existence was a passive one and his preferences were uncomplicated and subdued in the Continental manner. His sphere of activity had narrowed with time, and his wife could feel some compassion for him in his quiet tolerance of their shrinking wealth. As time passed, Mrs. Corey had assumed the complete management of their lives; and on occasion, she could regret that the costs of raising three children amounted to so much. If she and her husband had been alone, how luxuriously they could have lived in Rome on what it cost to maintain their Boston respectability.

Tom has investigated this paint business, his father continued, and believes it to be a wise choice for a career. Along with the possibility of his marrying the "paint princess," it may not be such a bad situation after all. Even if a match with the Lapham girl were imminent, Corey adds, what could be done about it? Unlike the English and Europeans, American parents can be consoled by the fact that they can do nothing about their children's marriages. We are too "delicate" to arrange their matches and when the whole thing is done, we remain silent for fear of making the situation worse. No, says Corey, the proper way for us in such matters is to discipline ourselves to "indifference." It is senseless to entertain feelings one way or the other about affairs in which we do not interfere.

Very often, interrupts Mrs. Corey, parents do take a hand in their children's marriages. True, counters her husband, but not enthusiastically and only to make it easier for themselves in case the marriage should succeed. My own suggestion, he says flippantly, would be to disinherit Tom. It would be uncomplicated as well as economical; but you would be against it, and Tom would be unruffled by the thing.

Corey agreed with his wife that society's attitude toward young people's marriages is faulty, but the present civilization rests upon it, he says, and no one is likely to begin a change. Parents would feel ridiculous going to one another and settling the marriages of their children. No, the best way, he concludes, is to avoid interfering altogether.

Tom returned home in the afternoon and related the particulars of his new position to his mother. I have consulted

Uncle Jim and he finds it a sound idea, he said. Mrs. Corey felt the pangs of betrayal at the idea of her brother's encouraging Tom with these people, but did not show any visible reaction. Young Corey spoke of his discussion with Lapham and the brief stay at the Nantasket cottage, to which Mrs. Corey responded a bit stiffly that she wondered what in the world a cottage at Nantasket might be like. They seem to be very good people, was his response to her next question, but they are only just now reading Middlemarch. I imagine that the "plain sister" is the one reading Middlemarch, Mrs. Corey speculated, to which her son offered only partial agreement. Yes, he said, it was the older sister who did the reading, but only in moderation. They seemed to have everything that money could buy, continued Tom, but then "money has its limitations." His mother came to discover the disagreeable reality of this fact more and more in her own existence and felt some gratification when she heard it directed toward the Laphams. Very true, Tom, she pointed out, "there is a place where taste has to begin." They seemed eager to apologize for not having more books about, the young man added. His mother seized the opening to establish that she knew "these moneyed people" very well; they poured out their wealth on all sorts of luxuries and then borrowed books from the libraries or purchased them in cheap editions.

Corey commented that the older daughter was "humorous," which confused his mother somewhat, and she shifted the direction of the conversation toward Irene's good looks. "She's a wonderful complexion," is all that Tom would allow in return.

Mrs. Corey confessed to her displeasure at the idea of her son in Lapham's paint business, but Tom reasoned that the important thing at present was the amount of money, and the fact that it was to be honestly earned. When Mrs. Corey learned that he was to begin work the very next day, she asked her son why he thought Lapham had taken him into the business so readily, when such a thing is usually difficult to accomplish. "And you don't suppose it was any sort of - personal consideration?" she asked cautiously. Tom did not grasp her meaning and Mrs. Corey allowed the matter to pass. In a subsequent conversation with her husband, Mrs. Corey remarked, "We represent a faded tradition." As long as a man's business is on a grand scale and his advertising decent, we do not really care; but we consider it a fine trait to pretend reluctance. Yes, continued Corey, I once thought myself something special and precious, but it is a relief to be aware now that you're like everybody else and can easily be replaced. As to Irene, the "paint princess," Corey admitted that the whole matter would affect him more personally should it come to a question of his son's marrying the girl. She is a good child, responded his wife, but it is a matter of her upbringing and I would prefer his choice of a wife to be of a different sort.

At the end of his first day's work, Tom Corey went down to the boat to see his mother off on her return to Bar Harbour. As he returned by way of the street and passed Lapham's office, he decided to fetch some foreign correspondence from his desk and tend to it at home. As Corey came to the stairway, he met Lapham and the pretty young typist who worked in the office. The girl had been crying, and he heard the Colonel say as she hurried off: "Well, then, you better get a divorce." At Lapham's prompting, Corey decided to postpone his work on the letters until the next day; and he and the Colonel walked off discussing another business matter. The next day Corey lunched with Walker, a balding and mustached bookkeeper of about thirty years of age, who was also employed in the paint company office. Walker commented on Lapham's business ability and also remarked on his employer's confidential and close-mouthed way of doing things. That paint of his, he announced, is like his very "heart's blood," and it's no joking matter with him. He's just too secretive about things, added the bookkeeper. That typist of his is an example. Walker referred to Miss Dewey, the pretty girl that Corey had seen with Lapham on the office steps, and said that he kept up a regular mystery about her, treating her as if she was some princess. She's probably had hard times, said Walker, and I have a suspicion she's been married. As the two men strolled back to the office, their conversation was interrupted by the sight of a drunken sailor and a woman arguing on the street corner. Suddenly, the woman shoved the man forcefully and he pitched over into the gutter. Pausing for a moment to see if he was injured, the woman bolted into the crowd. When they arrived back at the office, Miss Dewey had just finished her lunch and had begun her afternoon's work.

> **Comment:** Previously, we have seen Silas and Persis Lapham discussing themselves and their family as man and wife. In this chapter, the Coreys are placed in that same focus. They are not vicious people. Actually they are well-meaning individuals who are as concerned for the welfare of their children as the Laphams are for theirs. This is evidenced particularly in the two mothers. Persis Lapham cannot imagine Corey lowering himself from his social position to enter the paint business - unless it is being done with an eye toward Irene. This is agreeable to her, but she does not want her husband disappointed in his choice of an employee if Corey should not interest himself in their daughter.
>
> Anna Corey, Tom's mother, is apprehensive about her son's new position in the Lapham firm. It is not easy, she remarks to him, for a young man to make his way into these businesses. Why do you think Colonel Lapham took you on so quickly, she asks, unless there were "personal reasons." By this she implies an ulterior motive on the Laphams' part, namely, the matching of their daughter with the socially prominent young Bostonian. Howells had

a wonderful faculty for portraying women. Persis Lapham and Anna Corey seem little like characters in "fictions" (as Tom Corey referred to them). They are very believable women, each in her own station in life, and each with her personal and hereditary way of reacting apprehensively to her child's marriage.

In his conversation with his wife it is obvious that Bromfield Corey is what might be called a realist-at-a-distance. He is aware of the changes in the traditional social structure that are taking place and accepts them, but he prefers not to come face to face with them. The old order, as the socially prominent Bostonians knew it, was being crowded by the new force represented by Silas Lapham. The standards, "values," refinement, family, and ratified purities of social position are being forced into compromises with the coarser one-generation, self-made rich. It affects Mrs. Corey more than it does her husband, but in his droll philosophy and narrow, aloof existence, he can allow the rough disturbances of Lapham types and what they stand for to be less personal affairs and more distant academic concerns. Tom's entry into Lapham's business is a necessary compromise to financial necessity and the times; and we have seen that the elder Corey can even justify it on the grounds of characteristics inherited by his son from his own enterprising father, Phillips Corey. However, when his wife suggests the possibility of Tom and Irene Lapham marrying, Bromfield Corey admits that it would surely be a more "personal" thing for him then.

Even the interference of parents in their children's marriages seems an outdated thing to Corey. It is an old-world and futile notion for American parents to entertain. Times are changing; the standards by which people are evaluated are being altered. Money is everything; it is the new "romance," as Bromfield Corey remarked earlier, and in the quiet refinement of his leisurely aristocratic existence, he nods to the inevitable.

We have seen Tom Corey commence his business relationship with Lapham, and we have seen the young man growing independent of his heritage. Yet from time to time, he evaluates the Laphams and their standards by several of the social and cultural tests to which he has been accustomed. Two separate and distinct worlds stand before and behind him. He is the bridge between them, bringing what he can from the world of the Boston "Brahmin" to the shirt-sleeve materialism of Lapham's mineral paint enterprises. Howells is showing us that the crossover is a necessary one, for the isolation of the aristocrats is fast ending. It is not without uneasiness for all concerned, but on the whole it is a painless maneuver. Bromfield Corey's attitude of the inevitability of the situation is the voice of Howells foreshadowing the certain economic and social changes that were occuring, and would occur, in the latter part of the nineteenth century.

In this chapter our interest is aroused, and we are given some secondhand information about the mysterious Miss Dewey and her relationship to Silas Lapham. While the incident of the drunken sailor at the end of the chapter may seem to be of no significance whatsoever, we will be able to relate it to Miss Dewey and her employer as the plot advances.

THE RISE OF SILAS LAPHAM

TEXTUAL ANALYSIS

CHAPTER NINE

Silas Lapham was proud of his self-made accomplishment, and he made no effort to "lower his crest" before young Corey during the working day. Nevertheless, he was not above letting it get about the office that this was Bromfield Corey's son who had come to him for a position. Mrs. Lapham, however, would not allow her husband to bring Corey down to the cottage. We have our pride, and "I am not going to have them think we're running after him, but without any schemes."

Sometimes Lapham would take Tom Corey for a spin in his buggy, but this was the only "social attention" that he allowed him. They would talk business when the Colonel talked business and horses when he was so inclined, but these were nearly the whole range of the older man's conversation. On one occasion, they stopped at the new house and found Irene and her mother there. The young man and the girl spoke politely of the house and then touched carefully on such literary matters as they had all discussed on the evening of Tom's visit to Nantasket.

The example of *Middlemarch* arose, upon which Irene made a passable comment only to fall silent at the mention of another George Eliot novel, *Daniel Deronda*. As Irene nervously toyed with a wood shaving on the floor, the conversation seemed to work its way to the subject of Penelope, her literary opinions, and her good humor.

Irene then tells Corey that the family is going to have a library in the new house. After some speculation on the authors that should be present, Tom offers to compile a list of the standard writers that might be of use. We must get them in the attractive bindings too, Irene adds, I'll tell father "about their helping to furnish the room, and then he can't object." The two young people joke amiably about the wood shaving that Irene is trying to hook with the tip of her parasol and, with some mock gallantry, Corey presents it to her as if it were a flower.

At dinner that evening, Tom Corey discussed literature and the taste for it with his father. "I think I read with some sense of literature and the difference between authors. I don't suppose that people generally do," he guessed. His father had said that he imagined the general quality among "non-cultivated" people was rather low. It is difficult for us to imagine, his son observed, the "bestial darkness of the great mass of people - even people whose houses are rich and whose linen is purple and fine." The Lapham cottage was not exactly overburdened with good books, he says, but hastens to add that in certain ways they were conscious of their ignorance. The elder Corey suggests that it might be time for him to meet his son's employer, and wonders if a dinner might not provide the proper occasion. There is no obligation, responds Tom, and the father answers that since it is the summer season, at least there is no haste necessary in the matter.

In the house on Nankeen Square, Silas is puzzled by the way Tom Corey's father seems to "stand off." Persis hopes that he hasn't mentioned the subject to Tom, and Silas is furious at the remark. They are your friends, not mine, and furthermore, I don't even want to meet the man. However, he wonders also why they shouldn't make the "advances" without waiting for the Coreys to do so. I'm worth ten times Bromfield Corey's money and I earned it myself, he announces indignantly. We can't do it, replies Persis. They have been in society all their lives and you just cannot meet Bromfield Corey on "equal ground."

When Irene came home from the meeting with Tom at the building site, she carefully tucked the wood shaving he had presented to her into a drawer of laces and ribbons. Her sister caught her in the act, and the two girls joke and tease in their usual manner. Irene's affection for young Corey has increased, but she is desperately upset by the uncertainty of his intentions. As the two girls laugh over the wood shaving, Irene suddenly begins "to sob in sister's arms."

The next day Mrs. Lapham inquired of Penelope what Irene was doing with a wood shaving in her belt. After hearing the explanation, she wondered just what Mr. Corey meant by it.

Unable to reason out any certain conclusions about her daughter and the young man, Mrs. Lapham remarks apprehensively that "She really isn't equal to him, Pen. I misunderstood that from the first, and it's been borne in upon me more and more even since. She hasn't enough mind." Oh, she says, I wish we had never met those people, or decided to build the house and that Tom Corey had never entered the business - but we must bear the whole thing out now.

Comment: Silas Lapham is curiously bound between two forces. He leans toward a marriage between Irene and Tom Corey, that would certainly benefit his daughter, yet he cautiously and somewhat antagonistically approaches the topic of meeting Bromfield Corey. An understandable pride of self-accomplishment instinctively felt in the vicinity of spoiled aristocracy, boils up as a natural defense in this rough ungraceful man. More and more we shall see that the fading world of Bromfield Corey and the blustering presence of the newly rich are irreconcilable forces. As we have observed previously, the hope for some synthesis of the two ways of life lies in the figure of Tom Corey who incorporates ideally the qualities of both camps.

The meeting of Irene and Tom at the site of the Lapham's new mansion makes the girl all the more anxious about Corey's real intentions. We readily detect that what Mrs. Lapham pessimistically remarks later in the chapter is all too true: Irene is not equal to Corey, nor does she had "mind enough" for him. Her desire to attract him is leading her into an emotional involvement from which she will not be able to withdraw without great pain to herself and others. The wood shaving, insignificant in itself, is preserved by the girl as a tender momento. Irene, in her eagerness to create something where it does not exist, is grasping frantically at anything to represent a visible sign of Corey's affection.

Howells offers some commentary during the conversation between the elder Corey and his son.

A certain degree of ignorance flourishes among the "elite" as well as among those that are considered uncultivated, they suggest. The "bestial darkness" frequently hangs over the rich too. In his curiously realistic and resigned attitude toward life, Bromfield Corey seems to be suggesting that ignorance and a lack of discrimination are often discovered where you find them.

THE RISE OF SILAS LAPHAM

TEXTUAL ANALYSIS

CHAPTER TEN

....

Tom Corey was a likable young man. At Harvard and afterward, he was never reckoned as a brilliant fellow, but rather energetic and in possession of those "qualities of the heart" that endear a person to others. He had been somewhat aimless, yet showed the "smallest amount of inspiration" that can rescue a man from the charge of being average.

As the summer days passed, Silas calmed the architect's apprehensions by having only to "understand or feel the beautiful effect intended" to accept it - and be willing to pay for it. Silas had run the cost of the house to nearly one hundred thousand dollars, stimulated as he was with recent large profits on the stock market. His wife was wary, exacting a promise from him not to exceed that figure and advising him to stop playing about in financial areas unfamiliar to him. In an expansive mood, the Colonel revealed to his wife that his former partner, Milton Rogers, had been to his office attempting to borrow money. Silas proudly announced that he had loaned Rogers the money and had secured the loan with a block of stocks that the man had left with him. I did it, he says, and "I don't know when it's done me so much good to shake hands with anybody." Silas did not tell Rogers that he had been wrong in forcing him out of the company years ago, for as the millionaire told his wife, "I wasn't."

Persis is greatly pleased at what she says removes the one "speck" that had been on her husband, but she forced a promise from him that he would never press Rogers for the money.

On the following day Lapham brought young Corey down to the Nantasket cottage for supper. "Irene liked being talked to better than talking" and was satisfied to sit and "look pretty."

In the evening, the three young people sat on the veranda with Penelope monopolizing attention with her characteristic way of "running on" in a droll manner. From within the house, her parents could hear Pen entertaining Irene and Corey with stories; and Mrs. Lapham commented that she can never "feel down" when Pen is about. The Colonel added revealingly that he guessed that she had as much "culture" as anybody. As it grew late, Lapham encouraged Tom to spend the night but the young man discreetly declined. Strolling back along the road to the boat landing, Tom Corey heard himself cry aloud, "She's charming," and before he realized it he had unconsciously stepped off the path into the soft sand.

Comment: In chapter ten, Silas Lapham makes a fine gesture to satisfy his wife's troubled conscience about the Rogers affair. He swears that he feels no guilt about the matter and that there never was any "speck" on him because of the incident. Nevertheless, it seems that he is protesting a bit too much. Whether he is willing to admit it or not, the hand shake that

"done me so much good" had put some ointment on his own stubborn discomfort.

It is evident now in which direction Tom Corey's attentions are moving. The Laphams are as optimistic as ever about the young man and their young daughter, but Irene has lost Tom's attention to her witty and personable sister forever.

THE RISE OF SILAS LAPHAM

TEXTUAL ANALYSIS

CHAPTER ELEVEN

....

Upon reaching home in Boston, Tom Corey and his father discuss the idea of a meeting between the elder Corey and Silas Lapham. Bromfield Corey decides that he will go down to Lapham's office the very next day, now that he has taken the "bit" in his teeth. Tom reports that the Lapham mansion will be completed by the end of the year, and his father inquires facetiously if they will be important additions to society. Diplomatically, Tom replies that they are people of sound sense and correct ideas. Not enough, returns his father; those particular qualities for admission to society would bulge her ranks beyond belief. No, No, there is more to it than that; there are qualities involved "which may be felt, but not defined." They drink ice water, continues Tom. "Horrible!" replies his father, and adds that if they have not even given a dinner, how can they possibly be accepted into society?

In the morning, Bromfield Corey and his son arrived at Silas Lapham's office. After exchanging pleasantries, Lapham ran on at length about the favorable showing that Corey's son was making in the firm, extolling the merits of his paint as well as his own good judgment. Condescendingly, Lapham allowed that young Corey's education would not get in the way of his success in the paint business, nor as a matter of fact, would his upbringing. Bromfield Corey endured this, "triply armed in pride against anything the Colonel's kindness could do."

To Lapham's mention of the Events sketch written by Bartley Hubbard, the elder Corey's innocent but "Brahmin" reply is, "What is the Events? ... I read The Daily."

When Lapham arrived home that evening, he announced to Persis that Tom Corey's father had paid him a visit. Silas struggled within to maintain a nonchalant attitude about the whole thing, but it was a "stalwart achievement not to feel flattered at the notice of sterile elegance," and "not to be sneakingly glad of its amiability." He was probably the most pleasant man he ever met, said Silas; and he acted just like anybody else. The Colonel commented that the house should be coming along faster than it was, and his wife rightly detected in his impatience the desire to invite the Corey's to the new mansion as soon as possible. To her elder daughter Mrs. Lapham offered a puzzled "what do you suppose he means by it?" in regard to Bromfield Corey's visit to the Colonel. Perhaps your father is right, she added; after all, Tom Corey did seem to take a fancy to Irene last summer.

In the morning Colonel Silas Lapham is not well. Persis decides that he needs a day's rest and has word sent to the office that he will remain at home for the day. Penelope teases Irene about the possibility of a certain someone having to come down from the office to get instructions from their father, and Mrs. Lapham does not appear at all dismayed by the possibilities involved.

Tom Corey arrived at Nantasket on the evening boat to inquire about the Colonel's illness. In the course of conversation Irene is left alone with Tom and her mother hastens upstairs to encourage Pen to go down and ease her sister's nervousness. She'll have to start learning to manage it herself, Pen returns a bit sharply, but she yielded the point, waiting, however, until Corey was nearly ready to leave before joining the people below.

To her sister's question about her evening with young Corey, Irene responds that she has had a simply "splendid" evening - "We talked nearly the whole time about you!" With Penelope's kind encouragement, Irene's spirits are brightened about the possibility of Tom Corey's making frequent visits in the future. He has never mentioned Irene in the company of Penelope or her mother and the older sister wonders if Tom's visits are not the result of the slack social season in Boston. However, as he is more and more to be seen at Nantasket in future weeks, the apprehensions are lessened. Mrs. Lapham expresses her fears that the Coreys might think that Tom is being taken advantage of while they are away at Bar Harbour, but the Colonel indignantly rejects the idea. A reference to Tom's social "position" draws a furious thump on the table from Lapham and the threat to have a talk with this fellow if he thinks he can put on airs. He permitted himself to be subdued; and his pride, which had responded to Persis' observation, now restored itself to a calm at his wife's guarantee never to raise the unwelcome point again.

Comment: It is obvious that Bromfield Corey's visit to Silas Lapham is prompted by a desire to do the proper thing - and perhaps by a certain degree of curiosity toward the millionaire, paint-selling Colonel who had impressed his son so favorably and whose daughter might possibly become Tom's wife.

The meeting is not without some pain for the elder Corey. We must remember the sense of elegant purity that was the natural social atmosphere for this Boston aristocrat. How degrading it must be to have a coarse and ungrammatical hulk of a man praising his son as he would any efficient apprentice clerk. From his Bellingham Place seclusion, this is indeed a graceful condescension by Bromfield Corey. We can see once again the irreconcilable aspect of the individual worlds that the two men represent. Corey has not even heard of the Events; and even on a small point such as that, there can be no real meeting.

At home Lapham is again torn by the same struggle of pride and admiration that we have seen him experience before. He is flattered by Bromfield Corey's visit and any conscious acknowledgment of admiration for the man would be made, naturally, at the cost of the Colonel's self-respect. The same condition is present when Persis speculates on Tom Corey's social level in relation to his attention to Irene. Lapham wants the match to come off, but he is infuriated by the specter of social superiority in the young man.

Tom's evening visit to the cottage only serves to make his growing attachment for Penelope more evident. He and Irene talk only of her sister. Pen's reluctance to support Irene in her conversation with Tom reflects a natural but spiteless irritation on her part about having to advance her sister's cause with a man for whom she is developing a deep love. Her sisterly affection and good nature oblige her to comfort and encourage Irene in the end; and the sight of the younger girl's giddy fluttering about Corey's intentions, and her pleas at the young man's next visit, prompt the older girl to become Irene's crutch once again.

Mrs. Lapham now notices that Corey has never referred to Irene in any encouraging way. This is the sign that the Laphams should see as an indication that his affections lie in a different direction, if anywhere, but their wishful thinking and natural assumption that Corey would be attracted to the beautiful Irene have clouded their judgment. The lesson is that the "fiction" of the novels is not necessarily real life and the handsome young man does not always choose the beautiful young lady - sometimes, Howells is saying, he falls in love with her darker, shorter, less attractive sister.

THE RISE OF SILAS LAPHAM

TEXTUAL ANALYSIS

CHAPTER TWELVE

After leaving Bar Harbour, Mrs. Corey and her two daughters, Lily and Nanny, passed two weeks at Interval and then returned to Boston. The girls have met no one to satisfy their "taste" while away, and they are drawn to the matter of their brother with keen interest. Your father never wrote a word about the way this thing has been going on, observes Mrs. Corey. With much of Bromfield Corey's own attitude toward such matters, his daughter Nanny philosophizes that it would have accomplished nothing anyway and would only have worried her mother. Tom would have gone ahead she added, but her sister Lily questions whether their father really knows much about it at all.

She is really a nice girl, Mrs. Corey allows graciously, and quite capable about several things. We won't provide her with any reason for thinking we're against her, says Lilly, but her sister interrupted with, Oh yes we shall and her ignorance will be reason enough. She's not completely ignorant, grants Mrs. Corey fairly, but her daughter would allow Irene no credit at all. It was established by the three women that the most that could be done was simply to hope for the best and to make the best of a bad situation if it should occur. Lilly, because of her impractical "artistic temperament" had drifted out of the discussion and allowed her sister and mother to handle the affair with Tom.

When an occasion presented itself, Anna Corey opened the matter with her son. They discussed the Lapham girls, and Corey believed that his mother would come to "like the elder, when you come to know her." The words had the uncomfortable implication of an expected meeting, and Mrs. Corey soon alluded to the younger Lapham daughter, whom Tom politely praised for her great beauty and practicality. He returned to a mention of Penelope and appeared a bit distant as he smiled to himself about some private amusement. Later, Bromfield Corey suggested to his wife that Tom may not have made any commitment to the Lapham girl as yet, and may not even know how he really feels about her. If he does decide to make a commitment to the girl, adds Corey, we won't hear of it until after she does.

Fearing that the Laphams might think Tom's family disapproved of his business association with the Colonel, Mrs. Corey decides to visit the Lapham home on Nankeen Square - alone. Persis Lapham received her visiting card and was taken with an unexplainable spasm of fear and nervousness, which became all too evident during the visit. Since their last meeting the Colonel's wife had become aware of her own worldly ignorance, so that she was unable to meet Mrs. Bromfield Corey on "the former footing of equality." Irene was not at home, but at her mother's request Penelope joined her and their guest in the parlor. Anna Corey was rather baffled by Pen's droll wit and "pert" replies and quickly formed an ardent dislike for the girl. After some further conversation, Tom's mother thanked the Laphams for being so "very kind" to her son and acknowledged rather coldly that his family was "greatly indebted" to them. When Irene returned home, her sister and mother were still in the throes of unraveling the meaning of Mrs. Corey's visit. With her customary wit, Pen undertook an account of the past minutes.

Mrs. Corey returned home and reconstructed the visit to the Lapham's for her husband. Persis was very self-conscious, Mrs. Corey observed. Her husband, knowing his wife all too well, remarks that he is certain that she made the woman so by acting as an "accusing spirit." Mrs. Corey is particularly displeased with Irene's sister whom she finds to be a "thoroughly disagreeable young woman." However, Mrs. Corey reverts to her husband's plan for a dinner which would provide the proper social occasion for bringing the two families together - for appearance's sake. We must have them all, says Mr. Corey, but we must be careful not to make them think we're ashamed of the whole thing. It does present so many problems, sighs Mrs. Corey; and after entertaining further misgivings, she concludes that a dinner will simply not do.

Comment: We are given our first introduction to the Corey girls in this chapter, and it is only natural for us to make mental comparisons between them and Colonel Lapham's daughters. Lily is certainly the less impressive of the two sisters. She seems too finely bred for any long interest in the frank discussions and tribulations of her brother's "sordid" association with the coarse Laphams. She dabbles in collecting specimens of seashore life, but she seems unrooted in the practical world. Her delicate refinement seems like a type of her father's own delicate sensitivity but without his sharp philosophical cut. In Nanny's directness there is something of a refined counterpart of Penelope Lapham's droll bluntness. There is a part of Bromfield Corey visible in her too. Perhaps it is the realistic approach to her brother's relationship and a sort of resignation to the natural development of the situation as it will.

Despite Anna Corey's aristocratic snobbishness, she does feel compelled to be proper and fair toward the Laphams. She is pulled in several directions at the same time. On the one hand, she is aware of her traditional social position which, under other circumstances, would forbid any association with the unrefined newly rich types that were being found more frequently in Boston. Her good breeding requires her to display fair play to some extent, and her sense of superiority dictates a certain basic kindness and willingness to seek some redeeming qualities in those she feels are her social inferiors. This tendency to try and salvage something in the Laphams that can be pointed to, if not with pride then at least with a minimum of distaste, is motivated primarily by her affection and concern for her son. She respects his judgment and has relied upon his decisions on occasion; therefore she is uncertain just how to approach his suspected love affair with Irene Lapham. Understandably, her struggles with position, fair play, and personal affection are painful ones.

Bromfield Corey has not allowed the situation to penetrate his narrow and private "Brahmin" world too deeply as yet. His wife is immediately and deeply affected, almost from the start, and her anxiety is as pronounced as Persis Lapham's is about Tom's intentions toward Irene. We have noted before that Howells is remarkably skillful in the development of his female characters and we can realize with what tenderness, yet realistic honesty, he advances in parallel fashion the emotional involvements of the two mothers toward the possible actuality of a marriage between their children.

THE RISE OF SILAS LAPHAM

TEXTUAL ANALYSIS

CHAPTER THIRTEEN

With no reasonable alternative in sight, Mrs. Corey returns to the plan of giving a dinner for the Laphams. The question arises as to whom it would be advisable to invite in order to avoid as much awkwardness as possible. Mrs. Corey's brother, James Bellingham; other Bellingham relations; the Rev. Mr. Sewell and his wife; the artist Robert Chase, a distant relation; a Miss Kingsbury, a perennial guest at Corey dinners; and Mr. Seymour, the architect for the new Lapham mansion become the choices. Mr. Corey is concerned about having guests outside of the immediate family and has some misgivings about the whole affair. Tom Corey wonders if a simple family dinner might not have been wiser, but his mother mentions that the elder Corey had felt it might appear that they mistrusted the Laphams in a social situation. Besides, adds Mrs. Corey, a strictly family dinner might seem "significant." To her son's inquiry as to what she meant by "significant," she replies that she would not want the Laphams to make more out of his association with them than was really there.

Later in the evening, Tom approached his mother and stated that on second thought he would not want more to be made out of the acquaintance than was right, and so it would be best not to have the dinner at all. By that time it was too late, for Anna Corey had already sent the invitations to the Laphams. However, her son's concern for any possible misinterpretation on the Lapham's part cheered her considerably about the matter. Tom appeared more concerned about the affair than he had previously, and his mother was at least pleased that he should be giving some serious consideration to the interpretation that the Colonel's family was receiving from his attention to them.

Since Mrs. Corey's visit, Irene Lapham and her mother had been in the poorest spirits, with Penelope showing a decided gaiety. When the invitation arrived, the women were too nervous to read it and so the Colonel was given the task. There was much confusion as to just how to interpret the invitation, since Mrs. Corey's visit that afternoon had been dissatisfying all around. Penelope's reaction is to be expected; and when her sister pitifully misinterprets Anna Corey's snobbish attitude, the older girl breaks out in laughter. Pen then calmly refuses to attend and her family displays its social clumsiness by imagining that they can excuse her absence when they arrive. The note of acceptance is prepared by Persis Lapham with much uncertainty; but the thing is finally dispatched, and the family begins to face the ordeal of preparation.

The one most unnerved by the necessity of deciding on dress was the Colonel himself. He finally yielded to the wisdom of being fitted out for a dress coat - something, which he believed made him look like a fool. The question of whether or not to wear gloves presented the severest test for the millionaire's composure. After consulting books on etiquette, he was still at a loss about what to do. There seemed to be no end to the necessary preparation for the dinner; and he asserted that if it could be done over again, he would "say no for all of us." Unwilling to take any chances, Colonel Silas Lapham finally purchased a pair of gloves in a "saffron tint," according to the advice of the shop girl, who reported that as the most fashionable color.

As he moved restlessly about the house, Silas caught a glimpse of Irene in all her young radiance, so beautiful in her lovely gown. His warm fatherly heart was filled with pride, and he was certain that she would outshine every other person at the Corey's dinner on the following night.

As the Lapham's were leaving for the Corey's home, Penelope was bright and witty; but when her family had driven off, she ran upstairs and broke into sobs.

Comment: It should be evident that the Coreys, while snobbish, are not spiteful people. Whatever will occur at the dinner will be the natural and perhaps inevitable turn of events, prompted by what the hosts are and what responses to the occasion their guests freely provide. The Coreys wish only the right thing to be done, and Mrs. Corey is the one most concerned with the outcome of the affair. She enjoys that same endless uncertainty about the existence of a tangible relationship between the two young people by which Persis Lapham finds herself distracted.

The Colonel is particularly humorous in his confusion about attire, but we cannot help but sympathize with him for finding himself in a situation which is so foreign to his simple and unsophisticated ways. In its way, it seems as great a personal sacrifice on his part to prepare for and attend the dinner as it

was for Bromfield Corey to endure Lapham's clumsy flattery in the paint company office. Both situations require of each man a certain submission to what instinctively runs contrary to his nature, and both men are motivated considerably by concern for their children.

It is evident that Pen's flippancy conceals a very tender and sensitive nature, and her glib responses will not support her once her family has driven off to the Corey's. Mrs. Corey's unpleasant visit is not so easily rationalized by Penelope, as it is by her sister and mother, and her respect for herself and her family contributes toward her refusal to attend the dinner. Penelope would be all the more unhappy by being present at an affair suspected of being arranged to place the relationship between her sister and Tom Corey in a clearer focus. Her sharp tongue would be her natural defense, and she is keen enough to understand that this would work toward the embarrassment of all concerned.

THE RISE OF SILAS LAPHAM

TEXTUAL ANALYSIS

CHAPTER FOURTEEN

....

The Coreys were one of the last old families that remained in residence on Bellingham Place, and the lovely old house that Mrs. Corey's father had willed to her there was conceived with elegant classical simplicity. The Colonel was waiting in the reception room and recalled the stern directive by Irene that he was not to proceed to the drawing room without his wife. His hands were cased in his newly bought saffron-tinted gloves and, in his self-conscious manner, they hung down on either side of him "like canvassed hams." When Tom entered the room, the Colonel observed that he was not wearing gloves. Hastily, he pulled his own off and forced them into a pocket. When the ladies descended, the introductions were made, with Mrs. Corey presenting Silas as "General" Lapham. A suggestion that someone might be sent for Penelope in the dressing room produced a sudden quiet. Persis responded "at her bluntest, as country people are when embarrassed", and Mrs. Corey's reaction to the excuse was slight but noticeable. Two other guests had not come, and so Pen's absence balanced out the party.

Silas was to take Mrs. Corey into dinner; and as he moved toward the dining room, he felt himself gently but positively restrained. They entered the room last, with Silas accepting the procedure without knowing why it should be so. During the dinner, both Mr. and Mrs. Corey were completely at ease. In the conversation about the new Lapham mansion, Silas seemed to get on rather well with Mrs. Corey; and he was delighted to discover that the architect Seymour had been included among the guests. In the excursions into painting, social conditions, and popular novels, Silas tried to listen closely but only partially understood what was being said.

Colonel Lapham was not a wine drinker, but an early attempt to avoid consuming what was placed before him soon gave way to consideration of politeness and simple thirst. When the ladies rose to leave the room at the meal's end, the men remained; cigars were provided and a bottle of Apollinaris made its appearance. Colonel Lapham was beginning to feel expansive; and as he drank another glass of wine, James Bellingham sat down beside him and raised the topic of Lapham's own "96th Vermont" regiment during the Civil War. The philosophy of heroism and cowardice was discussed, and it is made known that Bromfield Corey participated in the Italian revolutionary campaigns in "'48." When the discussion touches on more theoretical points of heroism, Silas finds difficulty in following the train of thought. Then, in a bold effort to make his presence felt with better authority in the conversation, he launches into a war tale of Jim Millon, that soldier's unfaithful wife Molly, their baby daughter Zerrilla, and the way in which the young Union army corporal was killed by a Confederate bullet meant for Lapham. His audience is noticeably impressed but Silas' brain is rapidly becoming muddled by his wine drinking. Charles Bellingham offered him another glass of Apollinaris. Bellingham had been anxious to meet the Colonel for he surely expected the man to be something "original." Instead of Apollinaris, Silas drank some Madeira wine; and the men around him waited for the continuation of his story - but he could only stare at them with his mind a perfect blank. Following a thick and embarrassed silence, it was suggested that the men join the ladies and Silas returned to the other room still unclear as to what had just occurred. Several of the men, along with Lapham, retired to the Corey library where Silas' unaccustomed wine drinking finally took its effect and restored him to his habit of enthusiastic boasting. The men must come down to see his paint works, he bellowed. The horses he kept would surely interest Mr. Corey. He thumped his chair for emphasis and informed himself privately that Persis could not have been more mistaken than to suggest that he was unequal to this society. He complimented the men around him. He humbled himself with his good fortune in "hob nobbing" with such gentlemen. He was worth a million dollars. He had bought off his partner. His money was earned honestly. The minister, Mr. Sewell, must come to him if he ever needed money. His wife had torn up a check for five hundred dollars and substituted one for a hundred dollars just so it wouldn't seem that she was showing off - and what a joke it was on Mrs. Corey. Silas was about to bid the ladies good night when Tom Corey gracefully suggested that Mrs. Lapham was waiting below. The Colonel's purpose became uncertain for the moment, and he left the company without paying his compliments to the hostess.

In the morning, Pen did not come to breakfast and Lapham, with his head throbbing, left for his office without seeing her. Later in the day, he requested Tom Corey to step into his office. His typist, Zerrilla Dewey, tried to speak to her employer; but he told her he might stop by her house later. When Tom Corey entered the room, Silas faced him and demanded fearfully: "Was I drunk last night?"

Comment: The figure of Silas Lapham is a pathetic one in this chapter. The engaging quality of his rough, direct manner is brought to disgrace in

the unnatural setting of a Boston society drawing room. His drunkenness is unintentional but all the more clumsy for his inability to even realize its development. His position as an industrial leader and new breed of American capitalist tottered into mortifying boastfulness and a sickening effort at good fellowship before men who had never known his type of business sharpness nor sense of great personal accomplishment. Their strength lay in what Bromfield Corey told his son was that something "that may be felt but not defined."

He was beyond his depth; Persis had told him he could not meet Bromfield Corey on equal terms and her honest appraisal of her husband was a prophetic one. It should be remembered that the Corey guests did not take advantage of Silas' social innocence, and even Charles Bellingham's interest in Lapham as an "original," while rather condescending, was only a desire to see at close range one of these "practical fellows." In his drunken effort to prove his social capacities, as much to himself and Persis as to the Corey dinner party, he misplaces that passionate self-awareness and pride of the self-made man that would have checked his onrush into humiliation before these Boston aristocrats.

Howells has been more than compassionate for Penelope in omitting her from this scene. Almost in deference to her sensitive and intelligent spirit that would have been quickly caught up in the pain of her father's performance, he appears willing to keep the full weight of it from her.

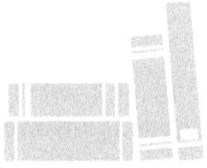

THE RISE OF SILAS LAPHAM

TEXTUAL ANALYSIS

CHAPTER FIFTEEN

Lapham has hoped feebly that he was mistaken about his drunken condition at the dinner party, but he quickly realized the truth when he faced Corey's "shocked and pitying" gaze. He inquired if they discussed him when he had left and Tom is forced to remind him that he was "among gentlemen" and that such things were not done in his father's house. In a burst of self-condemnation Lapham humbles himself before Corey in a string of self-accusations that force the younger man to plead with him to stop. "I have my reasons for refusing to hear you," Tom asserts. Silas continues to degrade himself before his employee and Corey is afflicted with a "repressed shudder for the abasement which he has seen."

When he took leave of the Colonel, Tom's sensitive, refined nature and his aristocratic pride, suppressed in recent months, asserted themselves in full force; and he was flushed with "contempt of the offensive boor, who was even more offensive in his shame than in his trespass." Then with a pang of remorse, he considered Lapham's innocent past and the fact that his pitiful self-humiliation sprang from a sense of guilt and contrition. He had shown bad form in treating Lapham the way he did, and in three hours time Tom Corey stood before Colonel Silas Lapham's front door. As he stood there it struck him how very far apart were the members of the two families; the particular contrast between his father and Silas had often been an uncomfortable comparison for the young man. His mother had made him aware of a possible injury to the Laphams by some misinterpretation of his intentions, and he had been emotionally uncertain ever since. With some humility himself, he determined to go before Lapham that moment, profess his undamaged respect for the man and seek to rectify the "want of sympathy" he had displayed in his employer's office.

> **Comment:** Lapham's abject grovelling before Tom Corey is ultimately the occasion that prompts a growth in maturity, responsibility, and heart for the young man. The tendency toward allowing the Lapham relationship to drift without a consideration of how it was being interpreted by that family is brought up short by the shock of the Colonel's upsetting apology. His mother's suggestion that he had an obligation to clarify matters in his connection with Irene only strikes him now with the full force of realization. Howells allows Tom's spirit a moment of torment between the secure haughtiness of aristocratic aloofness and a compassion for that simple family of whom he has grown so fond, and for whom he would now forsake "the stings and flashes of his wounded pride." It is a victorious moment for Tom Corey's character and while Bromfield Corey might disapprove of the proposed gesture from a "Brahmin" viewpoint, he would surely admire his son for a display of conduct that he himself would find difficult to match.

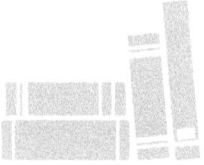

THE RISE OF SILAS LAPHAM

TEXTUAL ANALYSIS

CHAPTER SIXTEEN

Corey was admitted to the house at Nankeen Square by Alice, one of the Laphams' domestics. He was told that the Colonel was not at home, but that if he would wait in the drawing room, the girl would inquire when he was expected to return. Penelope was the only Lapham at home; and when she was told of Corey's presence, she tidied her hair and went down to meet him.

The Lapham's drawing room contained a tasteless assortment of inharmonious colors and grotesque statuary. Pen arrived and delivered Tom to the sitting room where it was the Laphams' custom to receive him. The couple enjoyed their easy way of running over an array of scattered topics. Pen mentioned *Tears, Idle Tears*, a book she had been rereading; and Tom observed that it had been discussed at dinner the night before. Penelope judged that the book was unnatural in some ways because of a female character who forsook her love of a man because another woman had loved him first. "Why can't they let people have a chance to behave reasonably in stories?" Pen questioned. After some uneasy conversation in which Corey intimated his affection for Pen, he blurted out that he loved her and that she must have known how he felt. "I thought - I - it was-" she stammered and held him off when he approached. He confessed to having come to see the Colonel; but that didn't matter now, he added. Pen was staggered by the revelation and begged Corey to go, telling him that she must refuse him without ever telling him why. The girl could not be comforted and exacted a promise from the young man that he would never try to persuade her or even come to the house again. As the Colonel's key was heard in the door, Pen impulsively embraced Corey and hurried from the room. When Lapham entered, Corey awkwardly explained that he had been waiting to see him but that it was late now and he would see him tomorrow. When the door closed behind Corey, Colonel Lapham advised himself that the very devil must have gotten into everyone tonight, and bellowed out to Alice for something to eat.

Comment: The taut climax of Corey's confession and the understandably mixed reactions that it caused in Pen are the inevitable result of the misinterpretation of Corey's attitude toward Irene, commencing from the moment the Coreys and Laphams met in Canada. Mrs. Lapham is strengthened in her belief that such a match is possible by a hopeful motherly concern and the slimmest possible evidence - or better no evidence at all. The uncomplicated Irene, with growing emotional attachment to Corey, wished it to be so; and the sisterly teasing of Penelope only makes it easier to misconstrue Corey's courteous and pleasant attention. Even Penelope, more perceptive than any of her family, has not guessed that she is

the one whom Tom Corey loves. Pen's reference to the unnaturalness of the fictional lover's sacrifice is certainly prophetic irony, for it foreshadows the very type of sacrifice she herself will choose to make within moments. Further examples of artful detail in Howells will be considered in the Question and Answer Section at the end of this Guide.

THE RISE OF SILAS LAPHAM

TEXTUAL ANALYSIS

CHAPTER SEVENTEEN

In the morning, the Colonel and his wife are the only ones at breakfast. Persis is told of Corey's strange visit the night before and is certain that the young man had come for no other reason than to speak to her husband about Irene - but his nerve had failed him. Later Persis goes to Pen's room where the girl is sitting before the window with evidence of having cried for some time. After a moment, she tells her mother that "Mr. Corey offered himself to me last night." With more "dismay" than amazement, Persis Lapham scurries from one alternative to another in her confusion. Irene was never "equal" to Corey, she admits, but "I couldn't say you had done wrong, if you was to marry him today." Before Pen's shocked response, she withdraws the statement and allows that Irene is a child and will "get over it." Pen is overcome with a sense of treachery on her part and cannot be consoled satisfactorily by any frantic search for solutions by her mother. Penelope's droll way of talking becomes a nervous response to the heartbreak she feels she has brought upon her sister, her family, upon Corey and of course upon herself. The

Colonel will have some answer for it, said Mrs. Lapham, and she passed the next hours in extreme discomfort. She had sent a message to Silas requesting that he come home early that day and his affirmative answer came as she was dining uneasily at noon with Irene. Irene was rambling on about wanting to buy one of those lovely pins that Nanny Corey had in her hair; and when Persis cautioned her about such enthusiasm until "he" had spoken more directly, the girl seemed crestfallen. Mrs. Lapham broke off and quickly encouraged her to go and buy the pin, by all means, "I should like to have Pen along with me," Irene suggested, but her mother advised against it right then.

> **Comment:** We can see once again in this brief chapter Howells' superb understanding of his female characters. Pen Lapham sees herself as her sister's betrayer and is willing to endure the very type of sacrifice she pointed out as "forced" and unnatural in the novel she was reading. Persis Lapham is driven into the torment of dilemma by her love for both her daughters and the inability to provide any positive advice, knowing that one or the other will suffer terribly. Pen's reaction shows great sisterly love and a reflex-like self-condemnation for the heartbreak that is to come to Irene. Her mother can muster neither heroic nor supremely wise solutions for the situation, and for her to do so would be a flaw in Howells' understanding of this simple and wholesome Vermont woman. Howells remarks of her:

> > The time had been when she would have tried to find out why this judgment had been sent upon her. But now she could not feel that the innocent suffering of others was inflicted for her fault; she shrank instinctively from the cruel and

egotistic misinterpretation of the mystery of pain and loss.... She was a woman who had been used to see the light by striving; and she had hitherto literally worked to it. But it is the curse of prosperity that it takes away from us, and shuts that door of hope and health of spirit.

THE RISE OF SILAS LAPHAM

TEXTUAL ANALYSIS

CHAPTER EIGHTEEN

When Silas arrived with the carriage, he and Persis drove off directly. They rode out toward the Boston suburb of Brookline, and Silas remarked that he had become more deeply involved with Rogers' business deals and that he did not trust the man at all; Persis would not speak of the matter. After some awkward hesitation on her part, she flung the news about Pen and Corey at her husband with a "Now are you satisfied?" He did not make anything out of the implication, for he quickly understood the distress and unhappiness that would prompt such a remark.

After some uncomfortable and unsatisfactory deliberations, the Laphams decided to seek advice from the Rev. Sewell, whom Silas respects greatly, rather than from Persis' own minister, Dr. Langworthy. The reluctant and embarrassed Laphams were received by Sewell, who thanked them "for trusting your troubles to me." When he had heard the Lapham's problem, he observed that an "economy of pain" was desirable in any such situation. We are deceived, he continued, by a "false ideal of self-sacrifice," and it is far better for one to suffer than for three to do so. You will all suffer some, he said; but your younger daughter will not die from it; and certainly, the guilt would be yours "if you did less." His advice was clear enough; Pen and Tom should not be deprived of each other for this unreal and un-Christian sense of sacrifice, the same type found so often, he hastened to add, in the deceptive novels of the day.

Comment: Silas and Persis Lapham appear in this chapter in all their unsophistication. There are no glib philosophic answers for them. They are parents conscious of their obligations, whose instinctive concern in this trial is only for "the children's good."

THE RISE OF SILAS LAPHAM

TEXTUAL ANALYSIS

CHAPTER NINETEEN

....

When they returned to the carriage, Silas said it was sound advice that the minister had given them. Yes, she returned rather bitterly, sound advice, but how would he like to have to take it himself. She added, gravely, that she knew the Rev. Sewell was right and that the thing had to be done.

Once inside the house at Nankeen Square, Persis overruled her husband's suggestion that he tell Irene and asked him to send the girl up to see her. When Irene entered the room, Mrs. Lapham wheeled about and told her daughter without any softening that Tom had never cared for her and that Penelope commanded his affection. To her mother's questioning cries about why she made no visible reaction to the shocking news, Irene responded plainly that there was nothing to say. She turned and made for her room, emerged a moment later, and entered her sister's room without knocking. She faced Penelope and presented her with several small objects, among which were the bright gold pin she had just purchased and a curled wood shaving that she had done up in ribbon. She dropped the pine shaving in her sister's lap without a word and over her mother's appeals, announced that she wished the Colonel to walk with her.

The father and his unhappy daughter started along together, the Colonel running on nervously and incoherently, and then maintaining silence at Irene's request. The girl bought some sleeping powders and announced to her father that she was going to visit the family's home town - renamed Lapham in honor of its now successful native.

The next morning Irene told her mother that she bore no hatred for Penelope: "She's never done a thing or thought a thing to wrong me. I had to let fly out at her last night; but that's all over now...." Irene brought Pen's breakfast up to her and after exchanging good mornings and not being able to commit to words what they felt, Irene returned to the lower floor and her housework. While they were preparing to leave for Lapham the next day, Irene asked her mother what answer Pen had made to Corey when he confessed his love. She forbade him to come here anymore, her mother said. Just before departing Irene went to her sister and directed her to tell Corey the entire story. You can at least say that we all thought he cared for me, she allowed. Rejecting her sister's embrace with gentleness, Irene swept out of the room.

When he had seen his daughter and wife off on the train, Silas returned gloomily to his business. Corey was anxious to see Lapham; and he waited until Rogers, who had been in the office, completed his business and left. Tom confessed his love for Pen without apology and swore that he had never been deceptive in any way to either girl. He asked if he might call upon Pen, and Lapham later told his wife that Irene's face passed before his eyes every time he was about to say yes. He believed also that Pen deserved some justice, and so he compromised by permitting Corey to see him, if he wished.

By her own admission, Penelope Lapham was feeling like a "thief that hasn't been arrested yet." When she received Tom Corey, she offered just a hint of compassion in a nervous smile that played rapidly across her face. She forgave him for "technically" breaking his promise to her, one which "had to be broken." She told him that they had all imagined he favored Irene, and he responded emotionally that it was never the case. Corey explained that the newspaper with the article about the Texas ranch was sent by his friend Stanton who was considering coming north to meet Irene. To Pen's protest that she cannot forget the hurt to Irene, Tom replies that they have done no wrong and have a right to each other. The girl's sense of pain and guilt persists no matter what young Corey says. He repeats that he has done no wrong and adds that he will wait until she changes her mind. When he tried to hold her hand she would not allow it. I cannot let you do that, she cried - not yet.

Comment: The Laphams and Tom Corey are now plunged into emotional involvement, and the suffering and sense of futility that they all endure is the whole substance of the chapter. Irene is no longer the tittering girl who was enchanted by a curled wood shaving. As she dramatically releases it into her sister's lap, Irene no longer seems the lovely romantic girl who tried to read significance into Tom Corey's every movement. In fact, the wood shaving with its pretty bow now seems foreign to her very nature. It is reasonable to suggest that Irene is in the throes of a painful movement from girlhood to womanhood. Her lovesick dream world is broken

and the realism of maturity is at hand for her. Her instructions to her unhappy sister to tell Corey what had occurred are marked with a sobriety not seen previously in the girl, and it is evident that we are not to see her innocent anxiety and rapture in the book again.

The very last word in the chapter - "yet" - is sufficiently charged with meaning to outweigh the rest of what Penelope had said to Tom Corey up to that point. The finality with which she addressed him, the resolution to self-sacrifice now seem not as eternally binding as they once did. With this single word Howells permits the possibility that Pen will yet accept Corey, if not without a completely guiltless spirit, at least in spite of it.

The appearance of Milton Rogers at Silas' office indicates that Lapham is still not free of this person. As he tried to tell Persis as they rode out toward Brookline, he was getting in even more deeply with the man.

THE RISE OF SILAS LAPHAM

TEXTUAL ANALYSIS

CHAPTER TWENTY

....

A week later Persis Lapham returned to Boston after leaving her daughter Irene in Vermont. I'd like you to take her off somewhere on a trip if you could, she remarked to her husband. Silas announced that he had to go out west on business and that he would be able to take Irene along. His wife asked him if Corey had been by and Silas said that he had. It amazes me, said Mrs. Lapham, that Pen is "willing to take the man that we all thought wanted her sister." I wish she did want him, replies Silas, but it doesn't look as if she does.

When Mrs. Lapham saw Penelope, the girl had already given up her crying and showed a flash of wry wit that was her curious way of expressing sadness at the moment. When she saw her husband again, Persis Lapham indicated her concern for Pen. She just sits there and broods, she said; and she doesn't even read anymore. Silas was rather preoccupied and announced that he would have to be off to the west on the following day. His wife realized that the business out there concerned Rogers; and when Silas told her of the difficult financial position in which his former partner had placed him, she expressed regret for having forced her husband to deal with the man once again. It's all right, he replied, "I was glad to make it up with him."

Lapham revealed that some apparently valuable milling property he had been holding as security for money loaned to Rogers was very possibly of little value, since a large railroad was considering buying it and could force the mills to be sold to them for whatever they wished to pay. In addition, Lapham's creditors had been pressing him for payments, while those who were in debt to him were reluctant to pay what they owed. Silas commented on Rogers' dishonesty and unpredictability and remarked that if things got worse, he was going to "squeeze" him. Persis was disturbed and was reduced to observing that Silas might remember that none of this would have occurred if he had not forced Rogers out of their partnership years ago.

In the evening of that same day, Tom Corey went to his mother's room to talk. He confessed his love for "Miss Lapham"; and his mother, discreetly and without enthusiasm, accepted his choice. Mrs. Corey, the genteel product of aristocratic breeding, made every effort to meet the situation with as much warmth as her emotions would allow. Tom reported that the Laphams had thought his attentions were being directed toward "the other sister." Mrs. Corey is amazed that such a misconception should have taken place. "To think," she continued, "that you could prefer that little, black, odd creature, with her joking and -" Her son caught her up short. Dumbfounded, he asked her if she had made the same error as the Laphams did; and she replied that of course she imagined it to be Irene that Tom had chosen. Irene was never anything but a "pretty child" to me, he confessed. Recovering her composure, Mrs. Corey tried to ease her son's upset condition and commented sympathetically on the terrible ordeal that it must represent for the Laphams. Tom spoke adoringly of Penelope's conduct in relation to her sister, and Mrs. Corey's love and concern for her son prompted her to praise Penelope and observe that the girl could not be expected to adjust to everything immediately. Tom requested that his mother be the one to inform Bromfield Corey, to which she agreed. She was a woman who "dwelt so much on decencies" and she instinctively proposed that she and her daughters pay their respects to Penelope. It's much too soon for that, Tom replied, hastily. It would only make matters worse at the moment. It was a source of relief for Anna Corey to realize at this moment that her husband was a man who registered little surprise even in extreme circumstances. He was a "sympathetic humorist" who could always include quiet amusement among his reactions to a given situation. Mrs. Corey was, however, surprised that he was able to laugh when she told him about their son's choice between the Lapham girls. His philosophic reaction was that time would manage to right the affair now that everyone knew who loved whom. Human sentiments adjust to human affections, he believed, and in response to the examples that he cited, his wife mustered a cry of "Bromfield, you're shocking!" "Not more shocking than reality," was his return. Mrs. Corey confessed her dislike for Penelope, and her husband added that he disliked the whole Lapham "tribe." She criticized him for opposing the affair now when he had not done so previously. He confessed that "as long as this crisis decently kept its distance," he was not personally disturbed - and now that it was at hand, his mind was still calm, but he felt himself unnerved. Yes, it was a very "awkward business," and everything must be done to help their son in this "terrible predicament." The Coreys weighed the undesirable aspects of the affair and at length they ended by conceding a certain degree of admiration and respect for Penelope.

Comment: In their own way, Anna and Bromfield Corey are as deeply disturbed by the unfortunate

love affair as are Silas and Persis Lapham. The reader should not condemn the Coreys' snobbery hastily, at least before reminding himself of the vast space that separates the worlds of these two families. Taste and propriety are the guiding principles in the Coreys' society, while a more unrefined, but equally governing set of principles that we might include under the phrase "doing the right and fair thing," are at the heart of the Laphams' sense of correctness. Mrs. Corey who, like Mrs. Lapham, never really knew what the children's relationship amounted to, is obviously making a supreme effort, at a cost to her sense of position and quality, to bring the affair to a happy resolution for her son. At the same time, she shows her good breeding in her concern for the feelings of Penelope's family in this emotional situation.

Bromfield Corey reveals himself in this chapter in a way he has never done before. He maintains a facade of urbane philosophy and an unhypocritical but aloof attitude toward life. He has never truly released the aristocratic contempt he holds for the Laphams and all that they symbolize. In quiet conversation with his wife, she understands clearly "the core of real repugnance that existed in his self-satire." We have remarked in the introduction that Howells knew Boston well. He understood the new self-made breed of man like Silas Lapham - and he knew that rarified creature, the "Brahmin" aristocrat of the later nineteenth century, who was still fed financially and aesthetically by a bygone time. In chapter twenty, Howells cuts to the heart of this species of American who, by his own choice, was sealed off from what he saw as an impure world.

THE RISE OF SILAS LAPHAM

TEXTUAL ANALYSIS

CHAPTER TWENTY-ONE

Lapham returned from his western business trip in two weeks and his employees at the office noticed that he was low-spirited and in a "sullen humor." At lunch that day, Walker, the accountant, speculated that Silas was in serious financial difficulty. It seemed to be a frantic situation for the Colonel, Walker thought, and he guessed that "that old partner of his has got pretty deep into his books." A one hundred thousand dollar house has got to be felt, he added, especially with the slump in the paint market. Corey had been more interested in his own private discomfort to pay too much attention to Walker's tale, but suddenly, the young man was taken with a splendid idea born of Lapham's possible ruin: he would offer the Colonel his own small fortune to bolster his sagging interests.

As the afternoon wore on, Milton Rogers appeared at Lapham's office. When Rogers was admitted to the private office, Lapham accused him of lying and deception in the matter of the milling properties. It was just as Silas suspected. Rogers took the charges with unruffled calm and then informed Lapham that he was in contact with an English party that was interested in buying the mills. The Colonel accused Rogers of lying once again, but ended by allowing the man twenty-four hours to produce the foreign buyers.

That evening after Persis had remarked how worried she was about Penelope's depressed behavior, Lapham confessed the seriousness of his financial situation to his wife. She blamed herself for the misfortune and said that she was certain they would always have a happy home, whether in Back Bay or in the Vermont town from which they had come. Silas described Rogers' plan to sell the mills to some English buyers; and after some deliberation, they decided that the Englishmen would have to be told about the threat to the mills by the railroad. Lapham still suspected that Rogers was lying; but if there was such an interested party, he would have to be honest about the risks involved.

Comment: We spoke earlier of the double meaning of the book's title: the moral as well as financial "rise" of Silas Lapham. Events are now unfolding which will make these notions most significant. Already, the downturn in Lapham's fortunes has prompted a moral temptation for him. Should he or should he not reveal to a buyer the potential threat to the western mills? To do so would only increase his financial weakness; to conceal it would contribute to his moral descent. The great wealth, which had previously secured him from the necessity of weighing moral values too heavily against financial ones, now seemed threatened. Not since he slackened his ethical standards and crowded Rogers from that early partnership had he been obliged to face a similar temptation.

THE RISE OF SILAS LAPHAM

TEXTUAL ANALYSIS

CHAPTER TWENTY-TWO

The Laphams received a letter from Irene, which failed to speak about her state of mind, but did remark about relatives and particularly her cousin Will. Mrs. Lapham speculated on the possibility of a match out there for her daughter, but Penelope said that whatever happened it would not alter the way she felt. Annoyed at this, Persis revealed to the girl that her father was in serious financial straits and that she might better pay some attention to comforting him than to dragging herself around in low spirits. Pen's reaction was to brighten up considerably and to tell her mother that she need not worry about her anymore. In the privacy of her room, she wrote a short note to Tom Corey, telling him not to see her until she sent him word; she had a special reason for requesting this, she said.

When Silas arrived home, he told Persis that the English buyers did not materialize, but that he thought he could survive financially without them. Pen was in lighter spirits than he had found her for some time, and the keen edge of her wit was a welcome relief, making her father laugh. That night they all attended a theatrical comedy, and Persis suggested to her husband that she believed it was "going to come out all right about the children."

Walker, the accountant, noticed the relieved atmosphere about the office; but the tensions came and went without any change in the Colonel's prospects. Lapham no longer discussed his difficulties at home and openly displayed his resentment at any "interference" by his wife. Silas concluded that the situation must be a burden on Penelope, but she replied that it only made it "easier" for her own problems. Pen wondered about the way Corey had obeyed her note so faithfully and thought of asking her father if Tom had taken sick.

When Silas began doing a great deal of paper work at home, his wife said she believed that he did not really know what his financial position was. Penelope often helped him with the figures; and they worked together, often until midnight. When news came that Irene was staying on in Dubuque and that relatives of the Laphams out there wanted her to spend the winter with them, Silas believed it was a fine idea and would do the girl a great deal of good. He often received letters from his brother in the west, who was watching the progress of events with the milling properties and the railroad. On one occasion, he wondered aloud to Persis if, without knowing for certain whether the railroad would threaten his property, he might rid himself of it as profitably as he could. Her answer was about what he expected, and he left the room disgruntled. In his haste, a single sheet of paper slid from his desk and rested on the floor. Persis Lapham understood it to say that her husband had paid several small sums of money over a year's time to a "Wm. M." She placed the sheet in her work basket, intending to return it to her husband when he missed it; but she did not think of it immediately after that.

> Comment: Chapter twenty-two is one of the shortest in the book but it advances the narrative in numerous ways: the possibility of a new romantic prospect for Irene lightens the Lapham's personal burden somewhat; Penelope is snapped out of her private depression by the news that her father is in the middle of business failure; Rogers does not produce the English buyers; Penelope is becoming anxious about Tom Corey; Silas is tempted to end his financial worries by compromising his principles and selling the western mill holdings without warning a buyer of the possible loss involved; and Persis discovers a curious bit of bookkeeping that Silas has misplaced.
>
> The reaction of Penelope to her father's distress is probably the most interesting revelation of character here. At first impression, it would appear curious that the girl should be cheered in any way by news of the family's near-bankruptcy. The psychology involved, however, is not really abnormal in any way. Just as Irene busied herself in a flurry of household activity after she learned of Corey's interest in her sister, so Penelope has seized her father's threatened ruin, and the comfort and assistance she renders him, as busy-work to relieve the weight of her own misfortune. Her attention to Silas allows her little time to brood over broken hearts.

THE RISE OF SILAS LAPHAM

TEXTUAL ANALYSIS

CHAPTER TWENTY-THREE

....

Over the winter, Silas and Tom Corey maintained only a business association. Since Pen's note, Tom had not been to the house, but Silas did not know of the arrangement made by his daughter. In the burdensome cares of his business problems Lapham did not take an account of Penelope's moods, although they scarcely eluded her mother's notice. Why don't they marry, Silas asked his wife one day after work. He knew the reason already and said that he thought it was "tomfoolery." If she would only marry him, Silas ventured, there would be some help in it for me. He could not look at his wife, and her reply told him she understood how hard-pressed he must be or he would never have been forced to say such a thing. In addition, the temptation to sell the mills, regardless of the ethics involved, still plagued him. When Persis inquired just how poor the situation had become, Silas answered that their nearly completed mansion had to be sold and that he had already shut down the paint works. He had been forced to do it because a West Virginia company had produced a good paint able to be sold for less than the Lapham brand.

When Persis found him in the sitting room later with his clusters of papers, she thought of the sheet he had dropped and the inscription, "Wm. M." To her inquiry about it, he answered that it was nothing, tore it up and threw it away. In the morning Persis discovered a stray scrap of it with "Mrs. M." written in her husband's hand. Who is Mrs. M. she asked later, but Lapham denied knowledge of any such person and the talk ended on a chilly note. At the office that day, Corey offered Silas his small fortune of thirty thousand dollars to help stabilize the business. The Colonel was deeply affected by the offer but declined, explaining that there was a stronger reason than ever now to refuse. As Tom withdrew from the office, Miss Dewey and an older, unsavory looking woman approached the Colonel's door. When he appeared, the older woman scolded him severely about "goin' back on me and Z'rilla" and their need of money for food and rent. When a call to the police was threatened, the two women left in haste.

Corey and Walker, the accountant, discussed the incident at lunch the next day, during which Corey defended the Colonel against the other man's insinuations. When the other employees had left the office Zerrilla Dewey approached Colonel Lapham with a problem. Her drunken husband has returned she says, and he and her mother were drinking heavily the night before. If she could only divorce her husband, Hen, she would be able to marry Mr. Wemmel, a fine gentleman who has been anticipating her freedom. Lapham promised to come over to Miss Dewey's rooms that evening, and at six o'clock he descended into the neighborhood of dilapidated barrooms and suspicious hotels where the young typist lived. Inside the Dewey apartment, Silas found her drunken sailor husband and the woman who had invaded his office, the girl's mother, who was trying vainly to conceal a bottle of liquor. In the course of the ensuing argument with the older woman, it is revealed that she is the unfaithful wife of Jim Millon, the soldier who saved the then "Captain" Lapham's life in the Civil War. Zerrilla is the little child about whom Millon was worried. Lapham had been supporting the two women for years, but now he tells them that the girl's husband, Hen, must get out or there will be no more assistance. On the way out of the building, Silas meets Milton K. Rogers and without a word goes off in another direction. At home Lapham confesses to Persis that he has lost heavily in the stock market and that he has fed too much money into Rogers' enterprises. Silas does not understand that his wife expected him to explain the mysterious slip of paper with "Mrs. M." on it. Persis learns that Corey has offered to help the Colonel financially and she is delighted with the opportunity to tell Pen such news.

Comment: Howells' sense of realistic detail is a conscientious one. As we approach the concluding chapters of the novel, he begins to piece together for us some of the odd bits and loose ends that had been so puzzling for so long. We now realize that Zerrilla's father was the same soldier who was the subject of Lapham's tale recounted to the men at the Corey dinner as his head grew befuddled with wine. We also recall that Tom Corey and Walker had paused for a moment one day as they returned from lunch to watch a drunken sailor and a woman arguing. The sailor, we suspect, is the good-for-nothing Hen Dewey and the woman who pushed him into the gutter, Zerrilla's unwholesome mother.

The mystifying "Mrs. M." whose unknown identity has been tormenting Persis Lapham is, once again, Zerilla's mother, Mrs. Millon. In addition to supporting the girl and her worthless parent, Silas had provided a job in his own office for his old comrade's daughter. This explains the curious bits and snatches of conversation

that Tom Corey heard passing between the girl and her employer from time to time.

The reader will still wonder why Howells places Milton Rogers outside the Dewey apartment. The answer will tend to justify Silas' estimation of his old partner's character and will in the course of events provide some additional fuel for Persis Lapham's growing suspicions about her husband.

THE RISE OF SILAS LAPHAM

TEXTUAL ANALYSIS

CHAPTER TWENTY-FOUR

....

That same evening, Mrs. Corey's brother, James Bellingham, discussed Silas with Tom Corey; Lapham had been to see Bellingham that very day. He had come at Silas' insistence to inform the younger man about the condition of the Colonel's finances and to explain the refusal of Corey's offer of financial aid. In the course of conversation, Bellingham remarks candidly that Colonel Lapham has "behaved very well - like a gentleman." Tom says that he is not surprised but his uncle is quick to reply, "I am. It's hard to behave like a gentleman where your interest is vitally concerned." When James Bellingham has completed his account of Lapham's present situation, the picture is a grim one; and the man pays tribute to Silas' character when he adds that the refusal of Corey's assistance must have been a great "trial."

At home on Nankeen Square, Penelope thinks that Tom was foolish if he thought she would allow him to give her father money and, she believes, affectionately, that the Colonel conducted himself twice as well as his young employee did.

Penelope was anxious about the fact that Tom had not tried to contact her, even though she had written him not to. After three attempts, she successfully completes a rather clumsy letter to Tom, beginning "Dear Friend" and closing with "Yours Sincerely." His return note is warm and affectionate. Tearfully, Pen writes to her love that he must not come until "this trouble" with her father's affairs has passed - if it does not pass, "all is over between us." When Tom advised his family of Penelope's decision, they admired the good conduct she had shown. His parents were in agreement. Their discriminating judgment concluded that she had "behaved well," and could not "possibly have behaved better."

James Bellingham had suggested to the Colonel that he declare bankruptcy, but the man's stubborn pride would have none of it. His credit grew shorter and it appeared to him that some of his creditors were conspiring against him. During these moments, he relished the thought of a bankruptcy that would discomfort those who were pressing him. Nevertheless, he could not entertain the idea for long, partly because of the thought of publicity that would follow a public declaration of his blundering. At last Silas resolved to sacrifice the unfinished mansion on the water side of Beacon Street. The real estate market was low at the moment, he was told, and there were several houses in the same area up for sale - and like the Colonel, the owners did not want their names revealed. When a buyer finally appeared, Lapham was reluctant to proceed with his plan. After closing the office one evening, he made his way over to Beacon Street in the hope of resolving his dilemma. He entered the tastefully designed mansion, catching the presence in the air of his Persis Brand paint. The floors were favored with an abundance of wood shavings, blown into clusters by a wind admitted through a tear in a linen window covering. On an impulse, Lapham lit a small fire of shavings and wood blocks in one of the hearths.

As he contemplated his situation, he was suddenly struck with an idea. If only he could raise enough money to buy out that West Virginia company that was beating down his paint prices, he would be all right. Yes. Why not? He just might do it. He was cheered immediately and did not hear the policeman who at first imagined him a trespasser and who was given a cigar for his trouble by Silas. When he had smoked the last of his own cigars, Silas Lapham left the still smoldering embers and went home, more cheerful than he had been.

At dinner, he was optimistic about the chances of pulling his finances through and he promised to tell his wife all about it in one more day. He was up in spirits that evening; and after he and Penelope had attended the theater, they decided to stroll over to see the new house by moonlight. Coming up to Beacon Street they were aware of great columns of dense smoke and the reflection of flames; Silas knew at once that it was their house. At home, Persis did not berate him but was afraid it would be thought that he had set the fire for insurance money. When Lapham discovered that he had allowed the policy to lapse and that the total investment in the mansion was lost, his wife remarked with relief, "Oh, thank the merciful Lord!"

Comment: It is interesting to repeat James Bellingham's estimation of the way Lapham is conducting his sagging enterprises. He "behaved very well - like a gentleman." Notice that Bellingham does not permit himself to say directly that Lapham is a gentleman, only that he behaves as real gentlemen do. However, this is a great compliment as well as a major concession from a member of Anna Corey's family. It does not seem that any of Howells' Brahmins are capable of saying any more than this of someone not of their "caste." In general,

Silas is "rising" to the occasions at hand. He seems to be proving the philosophy which maintains that a man's finest hours are discovered only in adversity, those times when his best qualities are forced into play. Certainly, the Lapham of the dinner party fiasco was a man in an unnatural climate, and as such could never thrive. The Colonel of unopposed financial success has his most memorable moments as an uncouth blustering braggart, so new to his wealth that he must occasionally announce the sum of it. If a man can mature after fifty, it might be said that Silas' character and values are maturing. He is a better man in his defeat and he is in the process of making that defeat a fine triumph.

This chapter also gives us an all too human picture of Lapham. His burning optimism about the chances of pulling through and its frequent change to gloom, his reluctance to dispose of "his hope for himself and his children" on the real estate market, and his sentimental but moving moment of isolation in the Beacon Street house. Persis Lapham's reaction to the loss of the house is curious, yet it should not be unexpected. In the Rogers affair, she has been ever mindful of the morally right thing to do. The "speck" she had seen on Silas disappeared when he loaned Rogers a large sum of money. Now, when the house is burned to the ground and there is a possibility of Silas being suspected of arson for the insurance value, she is thankful to God when it is learned that the policy no longer applies. The loss of the house is not as important as her husband's good name remaining free of "specks."

THE RISE OF SILAS LAPHAM

TEXTUAL ANALYSIS

CHAPTER TWENTY-FIVE

On the morning following the ruinous fire in his new mansion, Silas Lapham awoke to a sense of bleakness that made him regret the necessity of ever awakening again. The morning papers overlooked little in their account of the Colonel's misfortune, including the fact that the lack of insurance coverage would leave the financial loss solely in Lapham's hands. At the office that morning, he rationalized his situation as well as he was able. Since he had decided the night before not to sell the house, the loss of the insurance money really did not affect his present situation. He had simply lost something that he had not intended to use. During the afternoon, he arrived at James Bellingham's office and "dazzled" that gentleman with the boldness of his scheme to buy out the rival West Virginia company. Their funds are low, remarked Lapham, and they'll be eager for an offer like mine. Bellingham's reply was not so enthusiastic. He pointed out to Silas that they would have little difficulty interesting investors in their inexpensive method of manufacturing good paint. It would be wiser to sell out to them, was Bellingham's advice. Lapham would have none of the suggestion, and Bellingham was touched with compassion as he watched "this perversely proud and obstinate child fling petulantly out of his door." Lapham suspected Bellingham of being in league with all those creditors he felt certain were banded against him, and he resolved to prove to "high and low" alike that he and his family were independent. If Penelope and Corey had been engaged then, he reflected, he would break the thing. He would show people that he needed nobody.

Once in New York, Lapham went directly to the West Virginia company, who maintained offices there. They were "country persons" too and he got on well with them. With his "practical instincts," Silas wisely interpreted their enthusiasm as a lack of real knowledge about what the market held for their product and its power to enlist financial backing without difficulty. He proposed several plans with both parties, finally settling upon a merger. The West Virginians realized that they had a good product, but they also knew that they needed money. If Silas could supply the capital they needed, they would be just as agreeable to using his money as anyone else's. He would remain in Boston and manage the Lapham paint works: they would operate the New York office and their plant at Kanawha Falls. All that remained, they said, was the approval of their brother who was also a partner in their interests. They would have his answer in three days, and they assured Silas that he would most likely agree to the arrangements.

Silas thought that the price they had set for his investment was rather high, but he set about raising the capital he needed. Between the house on Nankeen Square and his Beacon Street property, he was able to raise thirty thousand dollars; he was a man cast into that "isolation to which adversity so often seems to bring men." Pride held him from returning to James Bellingham for more advice, and the fact that he had several days in which to raise his needed capital left the way to recovery still open to him.

Silas held several patents which Rogers had left with him as security. He had considered them worthless and was justifiably surprised when a gentleman came to his office and offered to buy one of them. Lapham incorrectly suspected some scheme concocted by Rogers, but sold the patent and was pleased to get even the lesser sum than he had allowed for it. He was again surprised when Rogers himself appeared in his office that same day. His former partner announced that the English buyers were in Boston and were anxious to see Lapham about the western mill properties. Indignantly, Silas asserted that he had no intention of swindling anybody with properties that might be worthless at any time. In fact, he did not believe that there were any such buyers, nor would they, if they did exist, make any substantial offer unless Rogers had deceived them. Rogers let it be known that he knew of Silas' attempts to borrow heavily, and his arguments in favor of at least meeting the Englishmen were persuasive. After a lengthy discussion in which Silas attempted every means to avoid meeting them, he finally agreed to join the foreign buyers and Rogers at eight o'clock that evening.

In the Englishmen's hotel room, Lapham wasted no time in announcing Rogers' dishonesty to them. He suspected that these buyers had been deceived by Rogers, and he set about correcting any ideas they might have entertained about that "rascal" and his honesty. The Englishmen were greatly amused by this ready American wit but pressed for a quick negotiation of the business. Silas soon suspected that Rogers and his English friends were allied in a scheme to purchase the mill interests from him and cheat the group of investors in England, who had sent them to negotiate the purchase. The Colonel decided to "think it over" and postponed his final decision until the following morning.

    Silas walked the way back to Nankeen Square, thinking all the while about the choice that had to be made. When he arrived home he was startled to discover Rogers conversing with Persis before the fireplace. He had expected, said Rogers, to find the Colonel there, but was discussing the situation with Mrs. Lapham because he wished her to be aware of an important consideration that he had failed to mention at the hotel meeting. He was destitute, he confessed; and the welfare of his wife and children rested on the success of the transaction with the Englishmen. Rogers pleaded and worked cleverly upon Persis' sympathies with references to the "Golden Rule" and "unchristian" behavior. Rogers' appeal stimulated mixed emotions in Persis Lapham. It was probably that her conscience was beset with pity for Rogers' family as well as a realization of the evil results that any dealings with the man would produce. She could be of no aid to Silas at this point. Realizing Lapham's moral reluctance to release the mill properties, Rogers suggested that he sell them to him and bypass any responsibility in selling them directly to the Englishmen. Legally, it was a safe negotiation. The Colonel smoked a cigar and wondered why he should not, he thought. He was holding back now for reasons that would not disturb anyone else. You will have an answer in the morning, Silas announced. Rogers remarked that there was no reason for such a sense of responsibility than when the Colonel was not so particular years ago. The remark struck home; but Rogers had put on his coat and left the house.

    In his office the next morning, Silas opened a letter from the railroad company and read their offer for the mill properties.

As he had feared, they were now forcing the sale on their terms; and another hope had disappeared. On his arrival, Rogers recognized immediately the futility of trying to persuade Lapham any further and cried out about the misery that would befall his family. When he was left alone at last, Silas wondered at the painful rewards for obeying his own conscience.

> **Comment:** Howells speaks of Lapham and the "isolation to which adversity seems to bring men." What is stated less explicitly, but with equal force in this chapter, is that along with isolation, the pressure of Lapham's temptation grows stronger as the state of his finances grows weaker. He is truly isolated, and this is necessary if the ultimate test of his character is to be a valid one. First of all, he has come to believe that all his creditors are in league against him; he even suspects Bellingham. This belief only makes him more determined to show them all that he and his family can win out alone. However, when the temptation to sell the milling properties confronts him, it is a different matter. From the time of Rogers' first visit about the English buyers until the letter arrives from the railroad company, he struggles to match his rationalizing against the direction of his conscience. His wife is there as a standard or test against which he can try out each proposed compromise. However, when he returns from the meeting with the English buyers and discovers Rogers in his home, he is forced to stand completely alone, without Persis; and the temptation appears to be the greatest. Rogers' arguments range from one of complete legal safety for Silas in the sale of the properties to one of compassionate appeal for wife

and family. The important thing here is that for the first time in the book, Persis is immobilized:

> Lapham stole a troubled glance at his wife, and saw that there was no help in her... Lapham glanced again at his wife; her head had fallen... she was helpless, now in the crucial moment, when he had the utmost need of her insight. He had counted upon her; he perceived now that when he had thought it was for him alone to decide, he had counted upon her just spirit to stay his own in its struggle to be just.

There is great irony in the fact that Persis is unequal to a situation that has followed almost inevitably from her constant pressure upon Silas to redress the wrongs she felt were inflicted on Rogers. In the moment of great spiritual trial to which her own moral consciousness has led her husband, Persis Lapham is "rooted in her old remorse...her perceptions...blunted and darkened...[but it was the fact that] she was silent against [Rogers] that dismayed Lapham."

A great pride is now born from this isolation which he now feels is total; and in the moments of final decision, his wife no longer has a place. She has forfeited that right in Lapham's eyes by her silence before Rogers.

THE RISE OF SILAS LAPHAM

TEXTUAL ANALYSIS

CHAPTER TWENTY-SIX

Later that morning, word came from the West Virginians that their brother had agreed to Lapham's terms; they now awaited him to fulfill his part of the agreement. His efforts at raising the amount necessary to merge his company with theirs only succeeded in producing less than half of the required amount. Still recalling the proud manner in which he had left James Bellingham's office, Lapham shamefully returned to discuss the situation as it stood. Bellingham advised caution and suggested that Silas visit the West Virginian's plant at Kanawha Falls before he attempted anything else. Lapham agreed to this advice. Before catching a late afternoon train to New York, Silas gathered up some papers in his office and scribbled off a note to Persis, telling her where he was going. The steam heat in the office was not functioning properly; and when he saw that Zerilla Dewey was affected by the chill, he suggested that she work in his private office where a small stove adequately warmed the room.

A short time after Silas had left for New York, his wife arrived at the office. She was contrite and unhappy about her failure to support her husband in his negotiations with Rogers the night before. She regretted not taking a greater personal interest in the business during the past year and thought of the time when she knew as much as he did about any part of it. Making her way past Tom Corey without notice, Persis went directly into Silas' office. When she discovered the pretty girl at the typewriter, she was annoyed that someone else should be close to him in the affairs that they once shared. The girl took no notice of her, and this disturbed her even more. The girl's replies to questions about Lapham were listless and rather indifferent, and she was only jolted out of her casual responses by Persis' announcement that it was Mrs. Lapham who was inquiring about the Colonel. Dejected in spirit and annoyed by the young and pretty girl that was sharing her husband's private office, Persis went home, wondering why he had never said a word about her. In the evening, a messenger delivered a note to the Lapham home. When Persis opened it, she became weak at the message's suggestion that she ask her husband about the young "lady copying-clerk" in his office; the note was unsigned.

Over the next day and a half, Persis' distressed mind worked itself into such a frenzy that when her husband entered the house on his return, she raced up to him and challenged him to reveal the identity of "that girl" in the office. Was she that "Mrs. M." on the scrap of paper she had found? Why did a respectable husband and father have anyone like that in the office? To her furious questions, he replied with another question, asking his wife if he had ever "accused" her of wrongdoing. She would just have to find out about "that girl" herself, he said, as he left the room. His wife screamed hysterically after him and fainted on the sofa. When she recovered, Silas had left the house, taking a traveling bag with him. When she finally located a "hack" on the streets, she was driven off in the direction of her husband's office. On the way she recalled her marriage to Silas, how she sacrificed for him, drove him along in business, and had been a faithful, loving wife for him. Besides, he had a guilty look when she challenged him.

When Persis rushed into the office, Zerilla Dewey leaped to her feet; and the older woman recognized her immediately as Zerilla Millon. The girl nervously explained that she was married and poured out the whole tale of her expectations of a better life with Mr. Wemmel and the Colonel's generous support of her and her mother all these years. Persis recalled how she had harangued Silas for aiding that wretched Moll Millon as long as she kept the baby Zerilla with her. She had made him pledge his "solemn word" that he would be done with them. Now, she realized how wrong it was to force a promise from him that would be broken because of his natural goodness and the debt he felt toward the man whose own death allowed him to live. After inquiring further about Zerilla and her situation, Persis started to leave the office. As she passed his desk, Tom Corey saw that she was weak and dazed and offered to accompany her to the carriage below.

As the evening approached and Mrs. Lapham had heard nothing from her husband, she asked Penelope to send word to Tom, inquiring about the Colonel's whereabouts. He returned word that he would investigate, and not long after arrived at Nankeen Square himself. The Colonel was at the family's home town of Lapham, she said, and would be there for the night and the next day. As Corey lingered intentionally to talk with Penelope they were startled by the sound of someone pulling the cord on the front doorbell. Both Tom and Penelope were amazed to see Irene, who had decided to return home when the Lapham relatives thought she had best be told about her father's difficulties. The moment of strained embarrassment was broken gracefully by Irene with the warmth of her greeting to Tom and Penelope.

When young Corey breakfasted with his mother the next morning, he made it known rather awkwardly that he thought now was the time for her to visit the Laphams. Anna Corey "mourned in silence" and responded to her son with "Roman fortitude." When she confirmed that he and Penelope Lapham were going ahead with the "affair," she agreed that the occasion had arrived for her family to call upon the girl. She must come here also, she added, and the relationship must be publicly announced without delay. Corey proudly explained to his mother Penelope's reluctance in announcing their engagement when her father was so hard-pressed financially; and he believed, he said, that it was time for the Coreys to make a graceful gesture. Politely, Mrs. Corey inquired about the Colonel's circumstances. She could offer no objection to her son's plans, unwilling as she was to deny, now, the expression of refinement and gentlemanliness that she had bred in him.

When Bromfield Corey heard the news, he laughed characteristically and was quick to identify his wife's discomfort as thoroughly ironical. She was now prevented from speaking openly about this detestable situation he said, by the very quality of refinement which demanded that she tolerate the girl in the first place. Seeing that his wife's sadness was unrelieved, Bromfield Corey rose to the occasion and expressed their mutual feeling about the proposed relationship. It had long disturbed her, and he had only mused philosophically while it continued to keep its distance. It was a "disagreeable affair," he asserted, and the Laphams are the least desirable family into which we would have wished our son to marry. They are "uncultivated" and show no possibility of improvement. Corey announced that he would accompany his wife on the visit to Penelope. They would still be hopeful about the relationship and would "behave" as well as their instincts and abilities permitted.

> **Comment:** For years Persis Lapham had chided her husband about the need to put things right with Milton K. Rogers. When Silas forced Rogers from the business, his wife saw this as a "speck" on his moral character. However, her scrupulous conscience enlarged his action into something more formidable and blacker than a mere "speck." Her attitude might suggest some hypocrisy when we consider her equally vehement opposition to her husband's continued assistance to Jim Millon's widow and daughter. She criticised this action because of the unwholesome nature of Moll Millon; but at the same time, she was unable to identify a different type of unsavoriness in Milton Rogers. This is not hypocrisy on Persis' part, for her preoccupation with the Rogers affair is typical of that fierce and narrowed conscience that blinds itself to anything but the single aspect of injustice or immorality that offends it most.
>
> We noted in the Comment section to chapter twenty-three that Howells uses detail significantly; we can see further proof of this here. After leaving the Millon apartment, Silas encountered Milton Rogers. Rogers had also been to Lapham's office several times and had seen Zerilla there. His reaction to Silas' refusal to sell the mill properties to the Englishmen was to send an insidious note to Persis suggesting an improper relationship between her husband and his typist. The incident of the "anonymous" note is the source of a calm rebuke by Silas for Persis' lack of faith in him. In the next and last chapter, Lapham remarks that perhaps Rogers actually believed him

to be involved in some affair with Zerilla, after all, he tells Persis, you did.

In this chapter, Irene returns home and her appearance is significant. It removes the final block lying between Penelope and Tom Corey. By her pleasant greeting to both, she indicates an acceptance of Corey's presence in the house as well as the fact that it no longer irritates old wounds. To her mother's almost apologetic remark that "It's the first time he's been here since she told him he mustn't come," she replies: "I guess it isn't the last time, by the looks..."

At the end of chapter twenty-six, we are given an opportunity to see the Coreys in the final realization that their son is to marry out of his proper "set." They are graciously resigned to what will be, and Bromfield Corey's outward composure is not disturbed beyond a frank statement of his unaltered attitude toward the unimprovable crudeness he beholds in the Laphams. We must remember that his intense class consciousness is severely wounded by the realization of this inferior match between his son and Penelope Lapham. In its own way it is as serious a blow to the Coreys as Lapham's financial tumble has been to him and his family. After all, Lapham's sense of self-made "position" rests upon his vast fortune and his rise from humble beginnings. The Corey's pride is not actually in money but in the tradition they represent and their ability to maintain their genteel heritage against all challenges. The Lapham marriage represents the most formidable challenge yet, and their calm but determined resolution to meet it with hope and refined behavior is not without its own species of heroism.

THE RISE OF SILAS LAPHAM

TEXTUAL ANALYSIS

CHAPTER TWENTY-SEVEN

....

When she returned from her stay with relatives, Irene let it be known that there was no romance between herself and her cousin Will. Persis Lapham immediately noticed the sharp change in her daughter's manner. She seemed severe and far less sensitive than she once was. No longer was she the dependent and impressionable young lady her mother had known. Irene had grown more durable by her difficult experience and perhaps her change was all for the good. She extracted the details of what had happened recently and was quick to understand the Colonel's predicament. Irene behaved with complete fairness toward her sister and Tom Corey, avoiding them as much as she could.

When Mr. and Mrs. Bromfield Corey and their daughters called, Penelope received them alone. She was certain that they entertained no misconceptions about the Lapham finances, and much later it was amusing to tell Tom with what uneasiness his parents had reacted to the grotesque statuary in the drawing room. Penelope and Bromfield Corey got on better than both of them had expected, with Tom's father finding her own nimble with something of a match for his own. Mrs. Corey was unchanged in her estimation of Penelope as intolerably "pert," but her husband found it possible to imagine his son's interest in her.

After three days, Silas returned home from his trip to Vermont. Persis made no immediate confession of her sorrow for misunderstanding him, for she was certain he would see by her conduct that their differences had been resolved. On his part, Silas acknowledged Irene's return with satisfaction and then confessed to his wife that he was declaring bankruptcy. He told her of the affair with the West Virginia firm and the fact that he had gotten an extension beyond the three days that they had allowed him at first. He had even brought a man up to Lapham with him to see the works. The man was wealthy and eager to invest in the paint company, but Silas felt obliged to tell him about the West Virginians and his own financial condition. The prospective buyer soon became wary of the transaction and withdrew his offer. It was Silas' "last chance," and he lost it.

Lapham brought the news of his final defeat to James Bellingham, who along with all those who were acquainted with the Colonel's affairs, confessed that his conduct had been admirable. The house at Nankeen Square and all its possessions were sacrificed in Silas' efforts to satisfy his debts. Those creditors whom he had at times suspected of being all arrayed against him, were now so impressed by his effort to make restitution that they offered to extend the time allowed. Were it not for the impossibility of opposing the West Virginia company, he might have continued his business much as before. However, he saw the futility of this and the Laphams decided to return to the town in the Vermont hills from which they had come.

Persis and her daughters found little at Nankeen Square to make them regret their departure, but Silas felt it most severely, experiencing what was "as much the end of his proud, prosperous life as death itself could have been." He still had the Persis Brand of paint remaining to him. It was too fine a grade of paint for his competitors to reproduce and the West Virginians did not attempt to oppose his manufacture of it. However, the old fire that had made him a splendid business success was gone. His bragging was stilled and Persis could painfully see that his great drive and energy had been blunted. Lapham was on agreeable relations with the West Virginians and through his recommendation, they brought Tom into the business.

Corey invested his money in the new company and had prepared himself for management of the South American affairs of the concern. Before his departure, he came to the Lapham's unpretentious Vermont home and implored Penelope to come with him. The girl was still torn by a sense of guilt in her imagined betrayal of Irene and maintained her refusal to marry Corey. Gradually, however, she lost the struggle to deny her heart. In addition to her attitude about Irene, she offered the reason of family poverty, the opposition of his family, and even a lack of personal beauty. It soon appeared, however, that she was only grasping futilely at straws that would not support her refusal any longer. Finally, she cried out: "Go, go! But take me with you!" Corey then returned to Boston to announce to his family that he and Penelope were to be married. Suspecting that she had sent Tom away on the basis of the old difficulties, Irene made certain that her sister had accepted Corey's proposal and that she was not sacrificing herself any longer. The marriage of Penelope and Tom was received without the "triumph" that Silas would once have known at such a match. For the Laphams, there was no sense of social betterment involved but simply the realization that their daughter had married the man she loved.

Lapham was a better man for his financial disaster. Without the social consciousness which had once weakened him, he again showed the sober strength and balance that had been his before the accumulation of great wealth. Persis could not rid herself completely of the feeling that Penelope's marriage was a little unjust, and thought of Irene with tender love and compassion.

For their part, the Coreys could summon no more than amiable tolerance for the Laphams. However, the Colonel's great display of character in the face of temptation and ruin appealed remarkably to Bromfield Corey's sense of the heroic and "finely dramatic," and he wrote Silas a letter of admiration. The Colonel's only reaction was that the atmosphere that the letter created might make it "more agreeable" for Penelope. Nevertheless, the distance between the two families remained unshortened. Before they departed for Mexico, the newlyweds visited the Corey home in Boston where everyone behaved as was expected of them. Bromfield Corey seemed to enjoy Penelope's droll manner: Lily sketched her, and Nanny was pleased to confess to her family that Penelope might round out to advantage in the "Spanish manner" and the substantial distance between them would now allow them to "correspond." On the whole, the Coreys were relieved that the marriage had not prompted the social associations with the Laphams that had loomed before Bromfield Corey with particular revulsion.

In Vermont, Colonel Lapham was promoting the small corner of the paint business which he still controlled and spoke with admiration of his son-in-law and the vigorous West Virginians who held the position in the market that was once his. When he encountered the Reverend and Mrs. Sewell during the summer after his financial collapse, he displayed an attitude in which he freely admitted his errors but showed a sense of pride in the awareness of his good conduct in the affair. At those times when her husband's "perfection" was almost burdensome to her, Persis Lapham would remind him of his foolishness in the stock market; he, in turn, would counter with a gentle reminder of her part in the Rogers business.

Mrs. Sewell had commented to her husband that she could not rid herself of a certain "contempt" for Penelope in Irene's disappointment. The Rev. Sewell maintained his belief in the ultimate justice involved in the way things turned out and ventured to assure his wife that Irene would eventually find her happiness with someone else. In fact, there was the possibility that the young West Virginian from the new paint company would take more than a casual interest in her.

Sewell was deeply attracted to the moral considerations that were involved in Silas' honorable resolution of his difficulties. The Laphams were reduced to the unadorned necessities in a home that was adequate, and Silas had reverted to a casual manner of country dress without attention to his personal appearance. He would say to Sewell that, on occasion, the whole calamity seemed to have been inevitable after the first trouble with Rogers. Sewell commented that the course of evil in the "moral world" is difficult to trace and often obscure to the eye. Silas still believed that it was questionable whether or not he was guilty of anything in his first dealing with Rogers. It was Sewell's contention that moral failures can often strengthen people for the "emergencies" ahead, and this he believed was the case with Silas. Sewell realized the great personal loss that financial failure had been to Colonel Lapham. He tried to discover what the man's true feelings were apart from the entire chain of rumor circumstances, and about the great moral decisions he finally made regarding them. Silas replied with deliberation that he sometimes felt a bit uncertain of his part in the thing. He was not altogether sure of the satisfaction it gave him, but that if he was faced with the choice all over again, he would probably do just as he had done.

> **Comment:** We cannot say that *The Rise of Silas Lapham* has a happy ending; realism allows for such a thing, but does not force it unnaturally from events. It is human nature to attempt to salvage some consolation from even the worst of happenings. In his tumble from great wealth to the rural Vermont from which he emerged, Silas Lapham can still take some pride in his good conduct. Howells allows Tom and Penelope the rewards earned by a wretched courtship, but it is obvious that the specter of Irene will not vanish for them altogether. Even Penelope's mother and Mrs. Sewell cannot rid themselves of a feeling of injustice in the marriage when they think of Irene. In this, Howells establishes the reaction as a more female one, for both Silas and the Rev. Sewell find it easier to see the justice in the marriage. In the matter of Corey's family, Penelope gains only a resigned acceptance, and there is little hope that the relationship will improve. Irene herself seems to be left without recourse to anyone or anything but the way to happiness is not shut positively; we can hope that Howells' suggestion of the West Virginian's interest in her may blossom into something substantial. However, this is realism too and it may not prove fruitful for Irene, just as such a thing is unpredictable in real life. The Coreys, whose dread of the necessity for social fraternization with the Laphams loomed up ominously, are at least consoled by the fact that the Colonel's "tribe" is in Vermont. Penelope is in Mexico with Tom, and therefore

the danger is removed to a safe distance on one hand and a secure one on the other. This series of checks and balances against perfect contentment or complete unhappiness is only Howells' reflection of the conditions of real life where the unrelieved extremes of human existence are excessively rare.

Even Silas and Persis exercise a balancing effect on one another. Whenever Silas swells with any self-satisfaction about his victory over temptation, he is reminded that his blunders were equally outstanding - nor is Persis allowed to forget her part in the Rogers incident.

There is no sudden resolution of events in this final chapter or in the book as a whole; to the contrary, the lives of all concerned go on with a natural accommodation to the circumstances in which they discover themselves.

THE RISE OF SILAS LAPHAM

CHARACTER ANALYSES

SILAS LAPHAM

At fifty-five years of age Silas Lapham seems destined to rise financially higher in his mineral paint business. Lapham is a self-made millionaire whose rough and uncultured Vermont ways cling to him and his family in their life in Boston. He is a thick-set man, with bold, roughly masculine features; his beard is reddish and short-cropped, and he has blue eyes. He is of medium height with large feet and huge hands like "hams." Lapham is fiercely proud of his wealth, the quality of his paint in which he has a near religious faith, and the fact that he is a self-made man. Despite his pride in his own accomplishments, he is attracted to the world of "sterile elegance" that is Bromfield Corey's. It is not an open and admitted attraction, for Silas understandably resents in the high social circles the very opposite of what his life and struggles have meant. The passionate dedication to idle graciousness is instinctively felt by Lapham as the natural enemy of his own energetic faith and business ability. Yet, the unassailable security of Boston Brahminism strangely appeals to him. It is perhaps the secret envy of a quality that does not rise and fall with the market, a something that cannot be bid for and purchased.

Lapham's great financial disaster is actually a spiritual triumph for him. His love for his wife Persis and his desire to please her in the matter of Rogers' partnership launches a series of financial difficulties that he cannot contain. It is probable that his love for his wife is even greater than they both realize. As his fortune declines she observes that it is all really due to the first dealings with Rogers. He tolerates this "last straw" type of remark unbelievably well for a man who has a capacity for fist-thumping emotional outbursts.

Silas is a good father and, with his wife, they both suffer during the strained love triangle between their daughters and Tom Corey. As financial ruin approaches, the boastful manner of the man subsides and he grows more humble and engagingly unsophisticated. His humility and high sense of personal integrity are not as evident in the days of his high prosperity. With the return to his Vermont origins, Lapham seems to revert to type, as though the blustering millionaire industrialist, who contemplated a Beacon Hill mansion, was only a fictional role into which he stepped momentarily. He is a finer man for his defeat and a wiser one because he can accept his situation without serious regret for having chosen the better part.

PERSIS LAPHAM

Before Persis Lapham married Silas, she was a schoolteacher and the match was considered to be to her husband's advantage. She brought to their marriage love, cooperation, an efficient business head for a woman of those times, loyalty and an uncompromising sense of justice and morality. Like her husband, great wealth has not deprived her of her practicality, a concern for extravagance, or her rural unsophistication. She exerts a great influence over her husband and commands his respect for her alertness to honesty and ethics in his business transactions. By the time his fortunes are declining, Persis has all but lost touch with the mineral paint business, and she regrets this considerably. She finds herself shocked to discover that her faith in her husband's personal morality has been so easily shaken by suggestion and her imagination, but she is supremely proud of her husband's ultimate victory over extraordinary financial temptations. She is no doubt prouder of him in his return to poverty than she ever was at the height of his business success.

Persis Lapham is a good mother, concerned for her daughters' future and realistically human in her neglect of the possibility that Tom Corey could fall in love with the plain Penelope. Understandably, she hopes for the social improvement of her children but she herself never seems to have been at ease in a world of great wealth and high society. Howells says of her that she "found it easier to leave it [the house on Nankeen Square] for the old farmstead in Vermont than it would have been to go from that home of many years to the new house on the water side of Beacon Hill." Persis is a remarkably stable woman. Certainly her acceptance of great prosperity and then financial ruin taken with unbroken stride, is not the least of the qualities which make her an indispensible companion to her husband.

Penelope Lapham is the elder daughter of Silas and Persis Lapham and the sister of Irene Lapham. Penelope, or Pen, must be considered plain in appearance when compared with her beautiful sister. She is shorter than Irene, darkly complected, but with a far better mind than anyone in the family. She is not rudely direct in her speech, but her sharp tongue is softened somewhat in a half sarcastic and half droll manner of speaking. Penelope is about twenty-one years old. She has literary tastes that help establish the early compatibility between herself and Tom Corey. She is a bright conversationalist and able to discover a humorous point in most anything she encounters. When Tom visits the Lapham cottage at Nantasket, it is Penelope who supports the conversation and animates the evening. It is her willingness and tender teasing of her sister's fondness for Tom that only serves to increase Irene's affection for him. We can see her selfless nature as she assists her sister and encourages her in an affair which commanded her own heart. Her willingness to renounce Tom for the sake of Irene demonstrates the fine depth of her character, although the feeling of melodrama is incompatibly close. In her unsophisticated, direct way, she greatly resembles her father; but in her seemingly eternal rejection of Tom for a sense of non-existent guilt, she is not unlike her own mother in that woman's overburdened attitude toward moral and ethical justice.

Penelope is really the salvation of the Laphams in the face of the Corey's sophistication. She is more than a match for Anna Corey's insinuations and a merry irreverent counterpart for the wry wit of Bromfield Corey. Like the rest of the Laphams, but certainly more evidently than her sister, Penelope can never be assimilated into Boston society. Moreover she has absolutely no desire to be, and is considerably relieved when the Corey circle is left behind, as she and Tom depart for Mexico.

Irene Lapham is the younger daughter of Colonel and Mrs. Lapham and the sister of Penelope. While Penelope is a generally stable character throughout the book, Irene's development falls into two distinct phases. Until the time when she realizes that Tom Corey loves Penelope, Irene is typical of the blushing, sensitive love-struck girl, so anxious to know the heart of the young man she loves that she subjects his every action and comment to agonizing scrutiny to determine exactly what he means. Everything, no matter how casual translates into romantic, significance. She is thoroughly unworldly and unintellectual. All that she has to commend her is a striking beauty which Howells observes is more pronounced for her superb coloring.

In her innocent love for Tom, she is the victim of a tragic misinterpretation of that young man's intentions. The blow falls upon her all the more severely because her immaturity did not allow her to see the relationship as anything but an ideal one. This represents Irene in the first stage of her development as a character.

After the illusion about Tom's love is harshly shattered, Irene is allowed to drop from the central activity of the book. When we see her again, having passed several months with Lapham relatives, she has changed considerably. The charming but somewhat tiresome innocence has vanished. Irene has, by her mother's own observations, hardened to life. The hard and unsympathetic jolt that she received forced her into womanhood by an unnatural process. However, this is **realism**, for maturity in life does not always arrive by easy stages. Howells remarks that what she has lost may not have been that important; however, it was important enough to produce a different person by its absence. Irene is now able to engage the family troubles as an adult, and her sister's affair with Tom no longer wracks her with a love-sick grief. She is scarcely more than her nineteen years when we see her again, but in another respect, the Irene that returns to Boston to assist in the family calamity is worlds apart from the slightly giddy girl who tied a bow on a wood shaving and placed it in her personal drawer.

Tom Corey is a handsome twenty-six year old son of a socially prominent Boston family. Harvard educated and eager to make his own way in the world, he is an example of the necessary compromise between the Brahmin idleness of his father, Bromfield

Corey, and the rough self-made captain of industry in the person of Silas Lapham. Temperamentally, he would not take well to a life of aristocratic inactivity, should it be financially available to him. His father notices the resemblance between Tom and old Phillips Corey who amassed the now weakened financial strength of the Coreys. Tom also inherited a flare for the world of business and the individual drive to succeed. He is not a brilliant young man, nor is his mind particularly quick. Bromfield Corey remarks that Tom is a trifle slow at times, sensing the meaning of something while his thoughts are still unclear about it. When the newlyweds are leaving the strained cordiality of the Corey home, Penelope's witty observation that now she will not feel strange among the Mexicans arouses only a "puzzled smile" from her husband. The elder Corey's remark appropriately comes to mind on this occasion.

In Tom Corey, the traditional reactions of a Boston aristocrat are still present, but not so as to stifle a compassion for Lapham and the pitifulness of his humility after the Corey dinner. His fine breeding instinctively rejects social inferiors but makes a harmonious alliance of the two worlds without the sense of revulsion experienced by his father. Tom is a gentleman. He is kind, charming, a good conversationalist, thoughtful, deeply upset by the hurt that has been done to Irene, yet is realistic enough to understand that personal happiness cannot be sacrificed for false sense of guilt. Not outstanding in any single characteristic, he likewise cannot be criticized for any recognizable fault. He combines the best of two irreconcilable societies and as such is pleasantly well-rounded.

BROMFIELD COREY

Slim, graying handsomely, clean featured, and elegantly tailored, he is a man "aloof from all the cares of the practical world, in an artistic withdrawal." He is the Boston Brahmin (socially aristocratic) son of a wealthy trader who has spent his fifty-odd years in idleness and artistic dilettantism. He lives upon the now dwindling fortune left by his father, and he is strengthened in his way of life by an unyielding awareness of tradition in refined taste, good conduct, and social prominence. In his idleness, he makes no effort to rebuild the family fortune and only gives an eye to certain economies in order that he and his family may live out their lives free of the necessity of ever working. He leaves the main concerns of the family to his wife, and his Continental refinement is appalled by the grossness of the Laphams. He is witty, sophisticated, charming, articulate and a master of dinner and drawing room conversation. He does not exercise his sense of aristocratic purity to the point of rudeness, but his utter revulsion at the thought of intermarriage and social fraternization with the Laphams is revealed in his private conversations with his wife.

Bromfield Corey loves his son very much, but the narrowness of his activity and his withdrawal from the brutishness he sees in the rising new-rich such as Lapham isolate him from any deeply disturbing concern for a possible romance between Tom and a Lapham daughter. He is affected only when the relationship becomes certain and the affair begins to touch him closely and personally. Temperament and tradition impel his ideas and actions. He can justify his non-interference in his son's concerns with the satisfying thought that affairs will take their course regardless of parental interference. He is a practically ineffectual man, who represents the very opposite of Silas Lapham, whom he comes to admire in a limited way for a type of moral stature of heroism. Beside the robust and active Lapham, uncultured but of tested and proven strength, Bromfield Corey seems little more than an aesthetic vegetable, with scarce resemblance to a productive human being. Basically, however, he is resigned and realistic toward life and fiercely logical to his aristocratic creed. He is constitutionally unable to imitate the practical vitality with which his father, Phillips Corey, was endowed and which his own son Tom seems to have inherited. His way is the way of the secure and isolated aristocrat, even though he understands that the days of such rarified beings are numbered. Still, he is unwilling to make more than limited condescensions and accommodations to such people as the Laphams. He and his wife do so only for appearance sake, for the sake of behaving as they expect themselves to, and out of an honest but impotent love for their son.

ANNA COREY

She is the wife of Bromfield Corey and the mother of Tom, Lily and Nanny Corey. Around fifty years of age, her life, like her husband's, has been nourished on refinement and a sense of obligation to position. She was formerly a Bellingham, an old and aristocratic Bostonian family. She is the actual head of the Corey household, for her husband's carefully guarded seclusion from the uncultivated in life has obliged her to assume the lead in family matters. Yet, she consults her husband and son on important considerations, as if instinctively wishing for the masculine authority that is absent.

Anna will never sacrifice her facade of refinement and aristocratic reserve to personal dislikes, and this is what supports the amiable stiffness of her relationship with the Laphams. Unlike her husband who permits himself no discrimination in his distaste for the Lapham "tribe," she is particularly repelled by Penelope, whose sharp tongue offends her with its wit and quick return. Despite her invincible snobbishness, she is keenly obliged to proper conduct even with those who are her social inferiors. Her relationship with the Laphams is a continual struggle between inbred reserve and the desire to terminate what she sees as an unsuitable match between Tom and Irene. What discomfort she endured at the thought of this marriage was relieved somewhat by Irene's beauty, but it becomes multiplied by the realization that it is Penelope, that "little, black, odd creature" that her son has chosen. Yet, this is not enough to jolt her from her desire to see Tom happy and her eternal attention to good behavior. In the very real pain she endures, she is only able to temper her politeness with implied disdain. Any open hostility would be a betrayal of all that was traditional and personal to her.

They were not "mean or unamiable people," says Howells of the Coreys; but Anna Corey, far more than her husband, is sorely taxed to maintain her habitual genteel reserve. She intends the Laphams no personal hurt; and, indeed, she is ever careful to avoid any appearance of shame or embarrassment at being associated with them. Her concern for the feelings of others reaches down to the Laphams in a compassionate way at times. Mrs. Corey's snobbishness is never really unkind enough to create more than the ill feeling it does when she and Penelope respond civilly but sharply to each other during her unaccompanied visit to Nankeen Square. In addition to her motherly desire for Tom's happiness, her sense of refinement restrains her from open opposition. She is unable to offer more direct and obvious interference in her son's affair for another reason. All the while she displays a reluctance to interfere, born of the hope that she will never be forced to dignify a relationship which her son will not carry beyond the bounds of polite acquaintanceship. In this she is mistaken, but Anna Corey will not compromise her position on any count. She is a lady and she knows it, and this is adequate reason for her to justify her conduct.

MINOR CHARACTERS

James Bellingham is a Boston businessman, socially prominent brother of Anna Bellingham Corey, and Tom Corey's uncle. He advises Tom to enter Lapham's paint company and later offers business advice to Silas about his financial troubles. He never goes so far as to accept Silas socially but holds a great admiration for his strength of character.

Charles Bellingham is a distant relation of Anna Corey. He attends the Corey dinner and hoped to find Silas remarkably interesting as one of those "original...practical fellows."

Miss Kingsbury is a perennial guest at Corey dinners, is interested in doubtful causes and comes well-equipped to engage in the sophisticated conversation of the dinner party.

The Reverend Sewell is the minister whom the Laphams met at the dinner party. Silas respects him highly, and he offers them advice on the heartbreaking relationship between their daughters and Tom Corey. Sewell is a fine gentleman who disapproves of the philosophy in modern novels as harmful to people. He comes to admire Silas for his great show of moral strength in the face of temptation.

Mrs. Sewell is also a guest at the dinner party; she tries to restrain her husband's eager tirade about the corrupting effect of novels. When Tom and Penelope are married, she cannot forgive the girl completely for Irene's heartbreak.

Mr. Seymour is a well-known Boston architect who has designed the Lapham's new mansion on Beacon Hill. He has the ability to politely cultivate and flatter the tastes of his clients and is also a guest at the Corey dinner.

Lily Corey is one of the two daughters of Bromfield and Anna Corey, and is Tom's sister. Like her sister, Nanny, she is every bit the daughter of an exclusive aristocratic family - and well aware of it. She shows little feeling or intelligence, and has inherited a poor copy of her father's dilettantism in her unfinished specimen collections of seashore life. Lily is considered too artistic for practical matters and is a weak female counterpart for Bromfield Cory's artistic idleness. She seems something of a sophisticated Irene Lapham at first, but with the book's progress, Irene matures sensibly while Lily gives no hint of ever improving beyond what she is.

Nanny Corey is the younger of the two Corey daughters and has a better mind and fresher personality than her sister. She is intensely snobbish with a directness of speech and sharpness of wit that provide certain bases for comparison with Penelope Lapham and Bromfield Corey. Both Nanny and Penelope are interested in literature, and their responses to life have a similarly irreverent flavor at times. Penelope, however, emerges as the superior character in her compassion for others and in the personal human warmth that Nanny and her sister both lack. Apparently incapable of any really tender capacities. Nanny, as well as the rest of her family, is quite relieved that all the Laphams are now at a safe social distance.

Jim Millon was a corporal in Silas Lapham's Union regiment in the Civil War. His life was unhappy, and he was eventually killed by a bullet meant for Lapham.

Moll Millon was the unfaithful wife of Jim Millon, who became his drunken and wretched widow.

Zerrilla Dewey is the attractive daughter of Jim and Moll Millon who had been given a typist's job in Lapham's office.

Along with her mother, Moll, she has been supported for years through the generosity of Lapham and the debt he believes he owes to Jim Millon.

Hen Dewey is Zerrilla Dewey's drunken sailor husband whom she wishes to divorce. Silas refuses to support him, in addition to Zerrilla and her mother.

Walker is the talkative and gossipy accountant employed by Silas Lapham. He often lunches with Tom Corey and discusses office affairs.

Bartley Hubbard is the sarcastic and haughty reporter for the Events, who interviews Lapham for a character sketch in the paper's "Solid Men of Boston" series. He reveals a noticeable fondness for pretty women.

Marcia Hubbard is Bartley Hubbard's gentle trusting wife. She considers Silas a fine man for sending them a jar of his Persis Brand paint and asks her husband not to ridicule him in the article.

Milton K. Rogers is the middle-aged former partner of Silas Lapham, taken into partnership when Lapham needed capital early in the business, and then forced out. He is essentially dishonest and continues to fail in business due to poor judgment and constant scheming. He maintains an "impartial calm" in the face of Silas' attacks upon his character and only becomes emotional when his financial ruin is certain. In his craftiness he is not above appealing to Persis Lapham's sympathy regarding his early removal from the business. The baseness of his character is seen in the anonymous note that he sends to Persis arousing her suspicions about Silas and Zerrilla Dewey.

THE RISE OF SILAS LAPHAM

CRITICAL OPINION OF THE RISE OF SILAS LAPHAM

When William Dean Howells sent an outline of his new novel to the editor of the *Century Magazine*, it was titled *The Rise of Silas Needham*. However, when the book was serialized in the magazine between November 1884 and August 1885, the events of the narrative and the character of Silas were moderated somewhat. In addition, the title was altered to *The Rise of Silas Lapham* and was retained in this form when the novel appeared in book form at the end of the serialization.

In the June 19, 1886, issue of *Harper's Weekly*, Henry James spoke of the book in company with Howells' *A Modern Instance and The Minister's Charge*. He remarked that he was struck with the "separation" between the novelist's "first cautious attempts" and these later, more powerful novels. In praise of *The Rise of Silas Lapham*, James observed that "Lapham, in particular, is magnificent, understood down to the ground, inside and out - a creation which does Mr. Howells the highest honor.... But everything in Silas Lapham is superior...." This novel had seemed to him "as the author's high water mark" until he had read *The Minister's Charge*, which he considered superior.

Howells' novels found favor with Mark Twain (Samuel Clemens) as well. He was particularly enthusiastic about *A Modern Instance*, writing in a letter to Howells that "You can never match this one." Mrs. Clemens found *The Rise of Silas Lapham* a satisfying novel and remarked that the book contained the best treatment of the "moral struggles of mortals" that the author had yet presented. She enjoyed the splendid portrayal of the characters, she said, particularly Silas and Persis, and liked them "in spite of their commonness." However, not all contemporary criticism was favorable to the novel. In an unenthusiastic *Atlantic Monthly* review at the appearance of the book in 1885, Horace Scudder took issue with Howells to the effect that the aspect of the novel concerned with manners was "shallow." He asserted also that the widespread unhappiness and suffering prompted by Irene's disappointment in love was simply "abnormal."

In our own day we have come to see Howells' great place at the head of realistic American novelists. Wallace Brockway says that *The Rise of Silas Lapham* is "Howells' claim to perfection and unquestionably asserts itself as a classic in pace, characterization, and adroit management of materials" ("Afterword" to Signet edition of *A Modern Instance*).

Carl Van Doren has said that Howells made "the most considerable transcript of American life yet made by one man." The particular aspect of this "transcript" in *The Rise of Silas Lapham*, takes place, as Marcus Cunliff notes, "before the spectacle of industrialized America had deeply stirred him. This is "his finest novel," continues Cunliff, and it

> **shows him at the height of his powers... A bare recital of the novel's themes gives no idea of its skill. High-minded in the kindest sense of the word, within**

its compass it is masterly. It flows; it is full of slyly observant, affectionate comment.

Rudolf and Clara Kirk see the importance of the novel in a transitional light also. They remark that:

> **Perhaps the greatness of *The Rise of Silas Lapham* lies in the fact that it was written just at the moment when Howells was turning from his earlier love stories to his later social novels. In the finished novel, considered by many to be his masterpiece, the psychological and the social interests are happily blended....**

A particular critical charge that has stirred up controversy about Howells has been one that detects in his presentation of reality, an apparent unwillingness or inability to confront the immediacy of evil. Edwin H. Cady has stated that the novelist never directly encounters "the violent and sordid facts of reality." This situation, he says, results from a "psychological breakdown" in youth, which reached into Howells' later life in the form of a "neuroticism." Critics do not always identify Howells' attitudes toward evil so handily. Harry Hayden Clark, in writing of *The Rise of Silas Lapham*, believes that

> **In the light of modern attacks on Howells as squeamish, it is well to remember that he said he refused to deal to any extent with illicit love not because it did not exist but because in American life of his day it was not habitual or representative of our people as a whole.**

Clark observes that Silas Lapham advises Zerrilla Dewey to divorce her drunken husband, but he adds that the **episode** casts a contrastingly attractive light on the other female characters in the novel. Clark's position certainly takes sharp issue with Cady's "neuroticism" theory, and maintains that we cannot "say that Howells was a Polyanna who closed his eyes to evil, either in the **realism** of manners or the realm of business." In relation to the ideas of social manners and business morals, Howells scholar Oscar Firkins sees an incompatibility in the parallel plots of the book. They are so unconcerned with one another, he believes, that they present an "irremediable check" to the movement of a great story.

During his own lifetime Howells witnessed a waning in enthusiasm for his writing. However, when an author is born in 1837 and lives to the dawn of the "roaring twenties," it is not altogether surprising that his work should suffer from one or more changes in the public literary taste. In 1915 at the age of seventy-eight, Howells had a manuscript returned to him for the first time since his late twenties; and it was, he wrote, "unconditionally refused." In our time, both scholarship and interest in the man are increasing. A glance at the name of Howells' critics in recent years will indicate that serious consideration of this great realistic American novelist is spreading beyond such stalwarts as the Kirks, Edwin Cady, and George Arms. If the appearance of a writer in paperback editions is a barometer of increasing popular interest, then Howells seems to be winning a new and substantial adherence. Certainly a major part of this appeal is to be discovered in his **realism**. Howells' particular aspect of realism is not that usually associated with the raw types of reality in modern fiction. **Realism** is not necessarily the portrayal of the violent or sordid in life. Harry Hayden Clark's observation that Howells refused to deal with the more unsavory aspects of life because they were not representative of the society as a whole is equally significant in a consideration of a rebirth in his popularity. As **realism** ceases to be automatically associated with violence and sensationalism, the quiet power of Howells' common, more socially representative reality will inherit what Henry James called his "really beautiful time to come."

THE RISE OF SILAS LAPHAM

ESSAY QUESTIONS AND ANSWERS

Question: Is the novel a realistic one?

Answer: In "The English Novel Since Jane Austen" Howells observed that "**Realism** is nothing more and nothing less than the truthful treatment of material." In *The Rise of Silas Lapham*, Charles Bellingham remarks that "The commonplace is just that light, impalpable, aerial essence which they've never got into their confounded books yet. The novelist who could interpret the common feeling of commonplace people would have the answer to 'the riddle of the painful earth' on his tongue."

These two quotations taken together give us a good idea of what Howells wanted to discover in the literature of **realism**. A "truthful treatment [of the]...commonplace" produces as nearly as possible a mirror reproduction of life. Howells, along with men like Henry James, rejected the idea of romantic idealization in literature. Howells, of course, is not without his streaks of the romantic but his art is essentially one of close attention to the common order and operation of everyday life. *The Rise of Silas Lapham* is a good example of this attention. It should be realized that close literary care for the common and average in life does not imply dullness or lack of inspiration. The brightness and significance of **realism** arrive with the "fidelity to experience" and action. This extraordinary only serves to detract from the realistic novel. By this, we mean that in **realism** the characters' actions and reactions should not tend to go beyond what might reasonably be expected of them and should not demand the use of our imagination for acceptance.

We may feel that there are a few too many coincidences in this book, but some careful reading will show that what seems convenient occurrences are not left isolated and hanging. Details are tied up and when this is done the events do not seem farfetched in the slightest. The course of events that we imagine continuing on beyond the ending of the book do not appear to reach a happy, satisfying resolution for all, even for a few, concerned. The characters' lives will continue naturally, flowing out of past events and into future circumstances with no promise of unreal personal and social forces manipulating them. Every character in *The Rise of Silas Lapham* is average. Silas and his family are wealthy but that is only a condition, and like anything else that may change, does not affect the portrayal of their common, human qualities. The Coreys are not unique people. They are average in their own class, and to the Brahmin eye they would be part of the society's crowd.

There is a hint at the melodramatic at times but on the whole Howells is loyal to his **realism** in this novel. It is this fidelity to the very details of action, gesture, and instinct in people of respective classes that animates far better than romantic idealization ever can.

Question: In addition to the realistic effect produced, does Howells use details in any other significant way?

Answer: The simplest detail is part of the honesty of **realism** that Howells labors for and there are innumerable examples of them throughout this novel. For instance, in chapter eleven, Tom Corey remarked to his father (of the Laphams) that he did not believe they had the habit of taking wine at meals. He hastens to add that he suspects them of drinking ice water when they do not have coffee or tea with their meals. The remark is left there and seems unworthy to be retrieved with any significance. However, later in the same chapter, after Lapham and his wife have been bickering about extending an invitation to the Corey's first, Silas "as if he could not endure that contemptuous atmosphere...got up, and his wife heard him in the dining-room pouring himself out a glass of ice water..." Such a realistic detail, is significant and forceful precisely because it is a painfully honest and unidealized representation. By the simple reference to a glass of ice water Howells links the two scenes, indicates something of society's standard of gentility, and exposes an aspect of the Laphams' ignorance of domestic refinement.

In chapters fifteen and sixteen there are also examples of this same use of detail. At the Coreys' dinner party, the course of conversation turns to literature and then, in particular, to the novel *Tears, Idle Tears*. Miss Kingsbury remarked that it was "perfectly heart-breaking." The Rev. Sewell observed dryly that "novelists might be the greatest possible help to us if they painted life as it is, and human feelings in their true proportion and relation..." The self-sacrifice portrayed in these novels, continues the minister, is foolishness. "Love is very sweet, very pretty-," he adds, "But it's the affair, commonly, of very young people, we have not yet character and experience enough to make them interesting."

In chapter sixteen, Penelope observes that the idea of self-sacrifice in *Tears, Idle Tears*, is "rather forced," in portraying one woman's sacrifice because another had cared for the one she loved first. "But it wasn't self-sacrifice - or not self-sacrifice alone," she continued,

> She was sacrificing him too; and for some one who couldn't appreciate him half as much as she could. I'm provoked with myself when I think how I cried over that book - for I did cry.

When we come to the actual revelation of his love by Corey, Howells automatically returns us to these random comments with a new insight and consciousness of the relevance which we now have. The ability to do so speaks eloquently for the technical beauty and great craft of the novelist.

Question: Is the novel autobiographical?

Answer: *The Rise of Silas Lapham* is semi-autobiographical. Howells was not a New Englander by birth, but his work in Boston provided him with much of the background for the book. Howells, like Silas Lapham himself, had rude beginnings, did not have an abundance of formal education and was a self-educated, self-made man and Silas was a self-made millionaire. The Laphams came from Vermont, the same state from which Howells' wife, the former Elinor Gertrude Mead originated. His conceptions of Boston Brahmins are not without source in reality. In his years in Boston on the *Atlantic Monthly*, he had ample opportunity to acquaint himself with the stratified society we distinguish in the book. Howells once facetiously remarked: "Don't despise Boston! Few are worthy to live there."

Question: What type of character does Howells portray best?

Answer: There is no doubt that Howells has created fine characterizations in the figures of Silas Lapham and Bromfield Corey. However, it is in dealing with the female characters that Howells excels particularly well. Among the novelists he read and admired, his "divine Jane" Austen had a strong influence over him in the aspect of his writing. She is greatly skilled in the delineation of women characters; and more than the ability to describe well, she maintains a mastery over the female psychology. Here, too, Howells is her splendid successor. Persis Lapham, Penelope and Irene Lapham, and Anna Corey are masterfully conceived.

If Penelope's sharp wit seems to hold off both author and reader somewhat, there is little if any of it in Anna Corey, and none in Persis Lapham. We know Mrs. Corey as well as it is possible to know the woman and still allow Howells to maintain her aristocratic bearing. Persis presents, it seems, the finest female study in the novel. With his attention to realistic reaction and instinct, Howells allows the reader to observe her mixed emotions towards her daughters' situations, never stereotyped nor even allowed to remain stiffly consistent. Her portrait is a very personal one. We can observe her curious approach to building the new house, an approach that cautiously denies what it really wants. We can see her pride, shame, and love for her husband, her deep hurt when she suspects him of misconduct, and a mute but eloquent contrition for her error that is understood more clearly by the man in not being declared openly and immediately.

Question: What is the meaning of the book's title?

Answer: The "Rise" of the figure of Silas Lapham takes place on two levels. First of all, it is obvious that the man has enjoyed an enormous financial rise. He has come from a Vermont farm to become a millionaire with the ability to begin construction of a great and fashionable Beacon Street home. Yet, there is another type of rise that Silas makes; and this one depends on his tumble from economic grandeur. This second "Rise" is a moral or spiritual one. As his business crumbles about him, and the fortune he amassed is grabbed away by poor investment and creditors, Silas Lapham develops a renewed moral integrity, one which his wife says he lost in early dealings with Milton Rogers. The lower his financial strength dips, the more awake his ethical awareness becomes. When the Lapham wealth is completely gone, Silas stands more admirably and independently victorious than he ever did before.

BIBLIOGRAPHY

EDITIONS

Cady, Edwin H., ed. *The Rise of Silas Lapham*. Boston: Houghton Mifflin Company, 1957.

Carter, Everett, ed. *The Rise of Silas Lapham*. New York: Harper & Brother, 1958.

Clark, Harry Hayden, ed. *The Rise of Silas Lapham*. Modern Library College Editions. New York: The Modern Library, 1951.

Kirk, Clara M. and Rudolf, eds. *The Rise of Silas Lapham*. New York: Collier Books, 1962.

The introductions to these editions are recommended as useful aids for the student's study of the novel.

OF SPECIAL INTEREST AND VALUE

Kirk, Clara M. and Rudolf Kirk. *William Dean Howells, Representative Selections, with Introductions, Bibliography, and Notes*. New York: Hill and Wang, 1961. American Century Series. This is a splendid anthology in many ways and devotes lengthy scholarship to Howells. It contains a

152-page critical introduction that is surely among the finest evaluations of Howells available, and includes a massive thirty-one page bibliography of scholarship to 1961. In selecting a broad range of Howells' writing, the Kirks have attempted "to relate [his] multifarious literary expression to his work as a novelist."

BIOGRAPHY AND CRITICISM

Kirk, Clara M. and Rudolf Kirk. *William Dean Howells*. New York: Twayne Publishers, 1962. Liberally flavored with much of Howells' own comment. Valuable biography and background for the student.

GROWTH OF HOWELLS AS A NOVELIST

Bennet, George N. *William Dean Howells: The Development of a Novelist*. Norman: University of Oklahoma Press, 1959.

Fryckstedt, Olov W. *In Quest of America: A Study of Howells' Early Development as a Novelist*. Cambridge Mass.: Harvard University Press, 1959.

EXCELLENT BOOK LENGTH STUDIES RESTRICTED TO CRITICISM

Cooke, Delmar Goss. *William Dean Howells, A Critical Study*. New York: E. P. Dutton and Co., 1922. See particularly pp. 243–249 regarding Silas Lapham.

Firkins, Oscar W. *William Dean Howells, A Study*. Cambridge: Harvard University Press, 1924. Consult pp. 111–119 regarding Silas Lapham.

HOWELLS AND REALISM

Cady, Edwin H. *The Road to **Realism:** The Early Years, 1837–1885, of William Dean Howells*. Syracuse: Syracuse University Press, 1956.

The Realist at War. Syracuse: Syracuse University Press, 1958. Any books and articles written by Professor Cady concerning Howells are to be recommended.

Cunliffe, Marcus. "**Realism** in American Prose" in *The Literature of the United States*. A Pelican Book. Baltimore, Maryland: Penguin Books, 1961. An interesting chapter by an English scholar that includes some comment on *The Rise of Silas Lapham*.

Kazin, Alfred. "The Opening Struggle for **Realism**" in *On Native Ground*. Doubleday Anchor Books. New York: Doubleday and Company, Inc., 1956. Abridged from the original Harcourt Brace edition of 1942. A good thirty-five page discussion of the early growth of **realism** and the place of Howells in it.

RECOMMENDED CRITICAL ESSAYS

Hart, John E. "The Commonplace as Heroic in *The Rise of Silas Lapham*." *Modern Fiction Studies*, VIII, 1963, pp. 375–83.

Trilling, Lionel. "W. D. Howells and the Roots of Modern Taste." *Partisan Review*, XVIII, 1951, pp. 516–36. This very important essay by Professor Trilling can also be found in *The Opposing Self: Nine Essays in Criticism*. New York: The Viking Press, 1955, pp. 76–103.

SOCIAL ATTITUDES

The following are recommended for their consideration of Howells' social opinions, an important aspect of his writing.

Arms, George. "The Literary Background of Howells's Social Criticism." *American Literature*, XIV (November 1942) pp. 260–76.

Bass, A. L. "The Social Consciousness of William Dean Howells." *New Republic*, XXVI (April 13, 1921) pp. 192–94.

Cady, Edwin H. "The Gentleman as Socialist: William Dean Howells" in *The Gentleman in America*. Syracuse: Syracuse University Press, 1949.

Hough, Robert L. *The Quiet Rebel*, William Dean Howells as a Social Commentator. Lincoln: University of Nebraska Press, 1959.

Lightning Source UK Ltd.
Milton Keynes UK
UKHW020739130320
360296UK00008B/107